Hearts and More™
Rotary Cut Appliqué

©2016

ISBN 978-0-9884279-0-7

Graphic Design and Printing by Palmer Printing Company
2902 South 3rd Street, Waite Park, Minnesota 56387

Published by
Sue Pelland Designs
4 Rockdale Hill Circle
Upton, MA 01568

suepellanddesigns.com

All rights reserved. No part of this publication may be reproduced or transmitted in any form or by any means, electronic or mechanical, including photography, recording, or any other information storage and retrieval system, without the written permission of the publisher. The written instructions, photographs, designs and patterns are intended for the personal, non-commercial use of the retail purchaser and are under federal copyright laws.

The author of and contributors to this book who compiled this material have tried to make all of the contents as accurate as possible. Neither the author nor "Sue Pelland Designs" assumes any responsibility for any damage or losses incurred that result directly or indirectly from the material presented in this book.

Classroom Use: Use of the projects contained in this book is encouraged as a base for classroom instruction, provided each student is required to purchase a copy of the book.

Introduction

When I started to quilt back in the 1980s, I was taught how to do beautiful needle turn appliqué. Over the years, I have gradually tried to find faster and easier ways to get my appliqué quilts finished. I discovered Mistfuse® and at last I enjoyed the look and feel of fused appliqué quilts. I still found that tracing my designs and cutting with scissors to be tedious. I set out to find a better way to cut vines and simple leaf shapes that I use all the time in my quilts.

In 2009 I invented the Leaves Galore™ templates and with them I introduced rotary cut appliqué techniques that changed the way we approach fusible appliqué. I wrote the book, "Rotary Cut Appliqué with Leaves Galore Templates" in 2012 as the ultimate owner's manual to teach quilters how to use the Leaves Galore templates.

Photo 1 shows five shapes that can be made in six sizes with the full set of Leaves Galore templates. The tools are useful for more than just appliqué. The book explains how to use the templates to design and mark quilting designs, make curve-edge quilts, and so much more.

PHOTO 1

The Hearts and More™ templates were introduced in 2013 to simplify cutting nine additional appliqué shapes. Photo 2 shows the nine new shapes and the range of sizes that can be made with just one of the four Hearts and More templates.

PHOTO 2

The following chapters will introduce you to the nine basic shapes that will become your building blocks for fusible appliqué. Then we will explore less conventional uses of the template such as marking quilting designs and using the tools for yoyos, clam shells, and drunkard's path quilts. A wide variety of quilts and projects gives you the practice and confidence you need to create your own rotary cut appliqué quilts. You will never want to cut appliqué with scissors again and you will wonder how you ever made a quilt without Hearts and More.

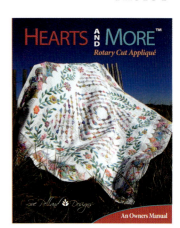

So get your supplies ready and let's have some fusible fun!

Table of Contents

- ♥ Introduction 2
- ♥ Chapter 1: Fusible Appliqué Basics 4
- ♥ Chapter 2: Tools that Make Rotary Cut Appliqué Fast & Fun ... 9
- ♥ Chapter 3: Master the Cutting Techniques: Cutting with One Fold ... 17
- ♥ Chapter 4: More Cutting Techniques 28
- ♥ Chapter 5: Special Quilts 36
- ♥ Chapter 6: Appliqué Stitching and Quilt Finishing Techniques ... 47
- ♥ Preface 52
- ♥ Project 1: Kaffe Clam Shell Quilt 53
- ♥ Project 2: Blue Moons 60
- ♥ Project 3: Yoyo Bed Runner 63
- ♥ Project 4: Mediterranean Blues 66
- ♥ Project 5: Sienna Rooftops 69
- ♥ Project 6: Candy Dish Pincushion 73
- ♥ Project 7: Drunkard's Path 76
- ♥ Project 8: Enough Love to Go Around 79
- ♥ Project 9: Row Quilt 86
- ♥ Appendix 92
- ♥ Resources 99
- ♥ About the Author 100

CHAPTER 1: Fusible Appliqué Basics

FABULOUS FUSIBLES

Years ago we wouldn't dream of making a bed quilt or show quilt with fusible appliqué. Fusible appliqué was known to be stiff and difficult to sew through. It was like quilting with cardboard instead of fabric. New generations of fusible products have changed my opinion of the quality of fusible appliqué and I now use soft, fabulous fusibles in quilts for my own use, for gifts, and for shows.

FABRIC CHOICES

The greatest drawback of fusible appliqué has always been the stiffness of the fused pieces and the chance of fraying along the edges of the raw edge fused patches. A very soft, new generation of fusibles minimizes the stiffness and produces a soft, snuggly appliqué quilt. However, with such a light-weight bond, fraying on the edges can be a problem. Cutting fusible shapes with a rotary cutter instead of scissors reduces fraying on the edges of the cut patches.

You can use any type of quality cotton fabric for fusible appliqué but my favorite appliqué fabrics are batiks. Loosely woven cottons will fray more than tightly woven cottons. Batiks are typically made with a higher quality, more tightly woven base fabric, making fraying less of an issue. I use batiks wherever I can, especially for raw edge fusible appliqué. Even with batiks, I always sew down the edges of my appliqué.

Enough Love to Go Around Brights. Made by Sue Pelland and Joanne Bertrand, Quilted by Diana Annis

When I am drawn to a beautiful printed cotton fabric for my quilts I try to use only high quality printed cottons. Printed cloth is only colored on the surface of the fibers. If you cut the fibers there is a white core. With raw edge fusible appliqué you might see that white core along the edges of the cut patch. When using prints I generally use a decorative stitch, such as the buttonhole or satin stitch, around the edges of the appliqué to enclose the cut edge of the fabric.

TO PREWASH OR NOT TO PREWASH?

Unless using precuts, I always prewash my fabrics. The primary reason is that I don't want my fusibles to misbehave.

Finishing chemicals on the surface of the fabric can interfere with the bond of your fusible. Textile companies put softeners on the fabric to make the fabrics in the store feel soft and smooth. Fusibles are made to stick to fibers and not to chemicals. These softeners prevent your fusibles from bonding securely so washing the softeners off the surface of the fabric to expose the cotton fibers is necessary. In addition, I do not want to take the chance of my fabric colors running or seams puckering because of uneven shrinkage. The recipient of your quilt may put your finished quilt through the washer and dryer so it is best to be sure your fabrics have already been machine washed and dried. Your quilts will last a lifetime or more so take time now to prewash and you will never be sorry.

No fabric enters my sewing room without prewashing. As soon as I get back from the quilt shop, I trim the corners of the fabrics with scissors, separate by color (light and dark) and run two loads through the washing machine. If I have very small pieces or really deep rich colors that may run, I swish them in the sink with a dab of hand soap or dish soap. Rinse until you can see the water is clear. Next, I run all fabrics through the clothes dryer on a hot cycle, remove when damp, and press. I do not use any form of starch or sizing when pressing. Use only a spray bottle with water to get out all the wrinkles as this will ensure the best bond possible. Now I know that everything in my fabric stash is washed and pressed so I can jump right in and start cutting my next quilt.

WHICH FUSIBLE SHOULD I USE?

There are many fusible products on the market today. Your choice of fusible can make or break your finished quilt. My favorite fusible for appliqué is Mistyfuse®. There are other soft products in quilt shops so do your research or experiment to find the one you like best.

You can use the fusible of your choice but I will explain the process for using Mistyfuse. (If you use another fusible, just replace the word "MISTYFUSE" with "FUSIBLE OF YOUR CHOICE.") Make sure you follow the manufacturer's instructions precisely.

Enough Love to Go Around, Brights

When writing this book, we made the black, white, and bright color version of Enough Love to Go Around. Pictures of the finished quilt are not in the book. After the quilt arrived home from the professional machine quilter, I placed the quilt in my washer to saturate the quilt with water in order to block the quilt. As soon as the quilt hit the water, the dark pink flowers and hearts ran so badly that by the time I got the quilt out of the washer, the quilt was ruined. I quickly over-reacted and started throwing bleach at the problem, completely changing the appliqué colors and ruining the quilt. This further reinforces my position about prewashing. I am not sure how this fuchsia fabric slipped through the cracks, but one bad acting square of fabric ruined a beautiful quilt.

If you have not yet tried Mistyfuse it may look a little intimidating at first. Mistyfuse comes as a lightweight, fibrous web with no paper backing. Use an appliqué pressing sheet or parchment paper to apply it to the back of your fabric. When using Hearts and More templates, appliqué shapes are cut without marking, saving you time. There is no need to mark so there is no need for a paper backing. You will be cutting multiple layers at once and the paper backing makes those layers slip. If you choose a fusible other than Mistyfuse, remove the paper backing prior to cutting with Hearts and More. With no paper backing to remove, the crisp, cut edges are maintained.

Avoid fusibles with a sticky side such as Steam-A-Seam 2. This type of fusible can't be folded and cut and can't be layered and cut after removing the paper backing. The cut edges will stick together with the gummy temporary adhesive. If you do not remove the paper, your fabrics will slip and you have to remove the paper from each cut patch, definitely not worth wasting your time!

Mistyfuse is available online directly from Attached Inc, from suepellanddesigns.com, or at your favorite quilt shop. It comes in white, black, and ultraviolet. It is available in a variety of sizes. I use white Mistyfuse in a 12" wide × 100 yard roll.

My ironing board is set up with a dowel that hangs underneath. I feed the Mistyfuse roll on the dowel so the fusible is always away from a hot iron when pressing. One hundred yards is a lot of fusible and a significant investment, however, Mistyfuse has a long shelf life and it will not go bad before using it all. Cutting with the Hearts and More templates is fast and fun and you will go through a lot of Mistyfuse. A Mistyfuse roll is a convenient way to purchase and store your fusible but only if you love it like I do!

APPLIQUÉ PRESSING SHEETS

Mistyfuse does not come with a paper backing so you must use an appliqué pressing sheet to protect your iron. You may already have one of these pressing sheets at home. It is sold as a craft sheet or a Teflon sheet and comes in white and brown. My favorite is the "Goddess Sheet®" made by Attached Inc. This brown Teflon and fiberglass sheet is extremely stable and durable and does not wrinkle, stretch, or warp. When using the Goddess Sheet there is a "Goddess Curve" on two corners. I keep the large curve on the bottom right hand corner so I know I am always pressing the same side. Both sides of the Goddess Sheet are the same but always using the same side minimizes the chance of getting fusible residue on your iron.

Appliqué pressing sheets come in many sizes. The "Fat Goddess Sheet" measures 21" × 27". It is generously sized to fuse an entire fat quarter of fabric at one time.

Parchment paper (not freezer paper) can also be used in place of the appliqué pressing sheet. There are two reasons I like the Goddess Sheet better. First, the pressing sheet is so shiny it transfers that shiny finish onto the Mistyfuse. The Mistyfuse is so thin and sheer sometimes it is hard to tell which side the fusible is on, particularly when using batiks. If you use the appliqué pressing sheet, the shiny side of the fabric is the Mistyfuse side. Parchment paper will leave a dull finish on the fusible, making it hard to tell which side of your fabric is fused.

Secondly, I like the appliqué pressing sheet better because you can see if there is Mistyfuse residue on it. Use an old credit card or a plastic kitchen scrubby to scrape off any bits of fusible. Fusible residue on parchment paper is nearly impossible to see so you risk getting it on your iron or on the next piece of fabric.

If you do use parchment paper in place of the pressing sheet, pin or tape the parchment paper along one edge of your pressing surface so you are always pressing on the same side of the paper. Run your hand over the paper each time to ensure there is no fusible residue that will get on the pretty side of your fabrics. After using the parchment paper two or three times, you will need to replace it especially if it gets wrinkly or ripped.

IRONS
For fusible appliqué I use a very inexpensive dry iron from a discount store. I like this iron because it is inexpensive, easy to clean, and has no steam holes that will leave unfused areas on my appliqué. If you get fusible on your iron, you can clean it off immediately with a used dryer sheet. If that doesn't work, try wetting a paper bag, then sprinkling it with table salt. Run the hot iron over the wet salt to take fusible off the iron.

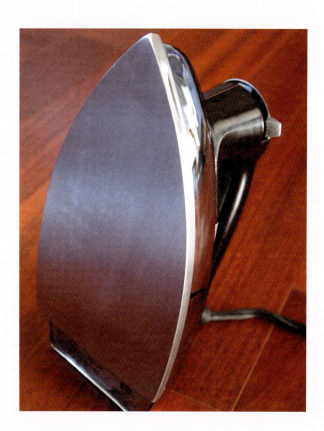

When fusible is really baked on, use the Bohin Iron Cleaner in a well-ventilated room. I clean my iron under the hood above my kitchen stove.

PRESSING SURFACE
I made my own pressing surface that is much larger than a standard ironing board. It is made from a sheet of plywood, covered in two layers of thin cotton batting, and a layer of cotton canvas. The board is attached to a metal shelf unit from a home center. This gives me a large, stable pressing surface that is not too soft and loads of storage below.

FUSING SUPPLIES
- ♥ Washed, dried, and pressed fabric
- ♥ Dry iron
- ♥ Fusible web of your choice, preferably Mistyfuse
- ♥ One or more appliqué pressing sheets
- ♥ Scissors
- ♥ Water in a spray bottle
- ♥ Large pressing surface

Applying Mistyfuse to Cotton Fabric: Step by Step

STEP 1: Set iron to cotton setting. Wash, dry, and press fabric. Steam as needed to remove wrinkles. Do not use starch or sizing.

STEP 2: Cut appliqué fabric to the desired size for the pattern and place right side down on a pressing surface.

STEP 3: Lay fusible web over the back side of the fabric. Mistyfuse has no right or wrong side. Cut Mistyfuse approximately $1/8$" smaller than the fabric to eliminate getting fusible on your ironing surface. (Photo 1)

PHOTO 1

STEP 4: Lay an appliqué pressing sheet over the fusible. Sometimes I use two appliqué pressing sheets, one on the bottom to protect my work surface and one on the top to protect my iron. (Photo 2) As long as you cut your fusible slightly smaller than your fabric there is no need for the appliqué pressing sheet on the bottom.

STEP 5: Smooth an iron over the appliqué pressing sheet starting in the center and working toward the edges smoothing as you go to eliminate air pockets. (Photo 3)

PHOTO 2

STEP 6: Wait 10 to 15 seconds for your pressing sheet to cool slightly.

STEP 7: Start peeling off the pressing sheet from one corner. Watch as you peel it off to be sure no fusible fibers are sticking to the pressing sheet. All fibers should be melted onto the surface of the fabric. If the fibers are stuck to the pressing sheet you have not heated the fusible enough. Repeat the process to heat the fusible again until it is securely attached to the fabric. You will see an even shine over the whole piece. If you see "spider webs" (Mistyfuse that is not melted), you have not pressed long enough. (Photo 4)

PHOTO 3

STEP 8: Lay the fabric over the back of a chair or lay flat with fusible side up. Do not fold fabrics or layer with fusible sides together until cooled for 15 minutes. After 15 minutes the fusible is no longer tacky and will not stick to itself. It is safe to fold fabric for storage or to layer fabric for cutting. (Photo 5)

PHOTO 5

PHOTO 4

CHAPTER 2:
Tools that make Rotary Cut Appliqué Fast and Fun

KNOW YOUR CUTTING TOOLS

The Hearts and More templates are extremely useful tools that work for a variety of end uses. For rotary cut appliqué, the combination of a 28mm rotary cutter, new sharp blade, mat, grips, and the templates all work together to make cutting curved appliqué shapes possible. Remove any one of these tools and cutting the shapes will be more difficult. The following is a guide to choosing the right tools for the job. Choose the best quality products you have available and your cutting will be easier to learn. The templates are also useful marking tools. I will give you several different marking options so you can find the method that works best for you.

SPD303 He Loves Me. Made by Sue Pelland, Quilted by Shirley Tetreault

HEARTS AND MORE TEMPLATES AS CUTTING TOOLS

The Hearts and More templates are 1/8" acrylic templates made for cutting appliqué shapes. Hearts and More templates come in four sizes: Templates A and B are included in the small set (HM1SM); Templates C and D are included in the large set (HM2LG).

All four templates are included in the full set (HM3ST). Template D is pictured below with a 3" and a 5" circle on the ends. The two circles are connected by a straight side and a curved side. The straight side is marked with capital letters and an orange band, while the curved side is clear with lower case letters spaced at even increments.

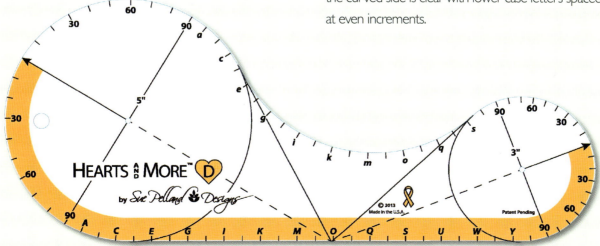

Depending on how you place the tool on your fabric, and what markings are lined up with the fold in the fabric, you will be able to cut various shapes with your rotary cutter.

Chapters 3 and 4 will teach you the specifics of each shape, but before you rush off to cut out your first fabric shape, please read this chapter to find out what all the markings on these tools are used for.

MARKINGS ON THE TEMPLATES

There are many markings on the templates that you can ignore completely until the time arises when you need them. Instructions in the following chapters will let you know when you need to identify and use each mark. A short description is provided here.

Each end of the template is marked with the size of the circle and a solid line that outlines the circle. There is a modified protractor on each end of each template. The protractor has an arrow in the middle pointing to the center of the half circle. The arrow marks the "ZERO" degree point.

From one 90 degree marking to the other, there is a solid line marking a half circle. If you place the two 90 degree markings on the fold of your fabric, you will be cutting a full circle. The measurement for the circle is marked along the straight line.

The arrow marks a quarter circle. Follow the arrow away from its point and you will see where it turns into a dashed line. Use the dashed line ending in the arrow to make straight-edge teardrops or flower petals by placing the dashed line on the fold.

Each quarter circle is divided into 10 degree increments from the arrow at Zero degrees to 90 degrees. These tic marks make it simple to adjust the shapes by 10 degrees at a time to make some shapes narrow or wide depending on your preference.

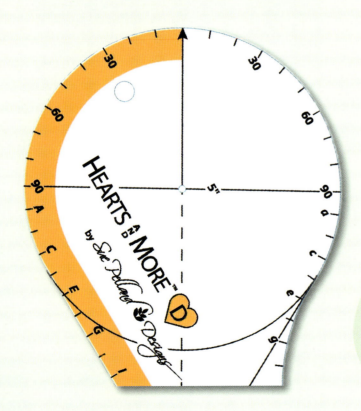

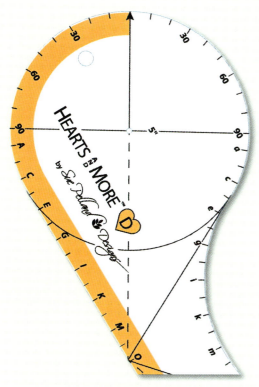

The third line identified is a solid line that comes off of the circle on the curved side of the tool and ends on the straight side. Hold the template so that one circle is on the top. When you look at this end of the template, the solid line forms a cone shape, with the half circle being the scoop of ice cream on the top of the cone. Use this solid line on the fold of the fabric to make straight-edge heart shapes.

The markings on the straight-edge and the curved-edge of the tool are not measurements. These tic marks are even increments but the increments vary by the size of the tool. On Template A, the smallest tool, the tic marks are spaced closely together. On Template D, the largest tool, the tic marks are more widely spaced. No measurements are made with these increments but we will use these markings as reference points when cutting certain shapes. Notice that the increments on the curved side of the tool are marked with lower case letters, while the increments on the straight side of the tool are marked with capital letters.

There is a small hole in the tool at the center of each circle end. Use this hole to mark the centers of your circles. You will find additional uses of this hole as you work with your tools.

ROTARY CUTTERS

It is best to use a 28mm rotary cutter to cut around the Hearts and More templates. Do not use a larger blade or you will cut or knick the edge of your templates particularly on the inside curves. Even with years of practice using the tools for cutting, I still occasionally catch the edge of the template with the blade. If you knick the template you can easily sand out the damaged area with a piece of fine sand paper or an emery board. If you do not smooth out the damaged area your blade will catch in that same spot each time you go past it when cutting. This can be frustrating! Take a moment to smooth away the sliver and your next cut will go smoothly.

It is imperative that you use a new sharp blade as often as needed. If the blade is dull it will push the fabric ahead of the blade and create ripples along the edges of the cut curves. This is not noticeable when cutting straight lines but very obvious when cutting curves. Recutting edges to clean them up takes time and mis-cut shapes are a waste of fabric, so keep your blades sharp!

Rotary cutters with a retractable safety shield and ergonomic style cutters do not work well. The retractable blade covers and ergonomic handles get in the way when cutting around curves. The stick style works best for cutting with Hearts and More. My favorite is the Olfa 28mm rotary cutter.

Many people like using an 18mm rotary cutter. These are wonderful around the curves and work great for cutting one or two layers of fabric. With Hearts and More we are generally cutting two layers at once. Give your 18mm rotary cutter a try. There are some shapes cut with four layers of fabric. If you always want to get a clean cut through two to four layers, use the 28mm rotary cutter instead. Once you master the technique, this rotary cutter will be more useful than the 18mm.

The most common cutting problems my students have are caused by dull blades. A sharp blade will eliminate many technical problems like rough cut edges. Even when my students know they have a sharp blade, this is the first thing I have them change if they have trouble cutting. The blade can be older than you think, it can be installed incorrectly, or maybe it is the wrong blade for your brand of cutter.

Refer to the cutter instructions and make sure your blade is installed properly with all the parts in the right order. Two blades in your rotary cutter is another common problem noticed in class. The blades often come two to a package stuck together with a bit of oil and it is easy to install two blades by mistake.

All blades are not interchangeable. Make sure you buy the correct replacement blades for your brand of cutter. The center holes have different shapes. The wrong brand of blade may not turn correctly in your cutter. If you are having trouble cutting, you may want to try a friend's 28mm rotary cutter to see if the trouble comes from the tool or the operator!

HOLDING YOUR ROTARY CUTTER

When using my rotary cutter, I hold it differently than most people. This helps me get better cuts around the curves. I place the butt of the rotary cutter handle in the palm of my hand, (Photo 1) and wrap my ring and pinky finger around it to keep it there. (Photo 2) Doing this keeps the rotary cutter in line with my arm as if it were an extension of my arm. Holding it in this manner allows me to hold the blade at a right angle to my template and my mat. This also gives me more leverage as I can lean into the cut with my weight rather than pressing down with my wrist.

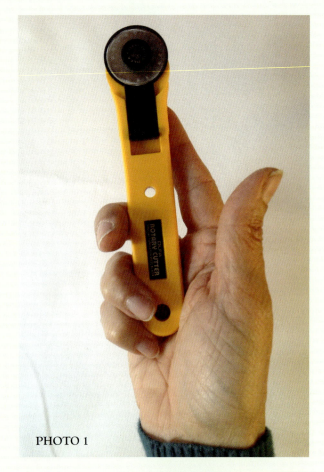

PHOTO 1

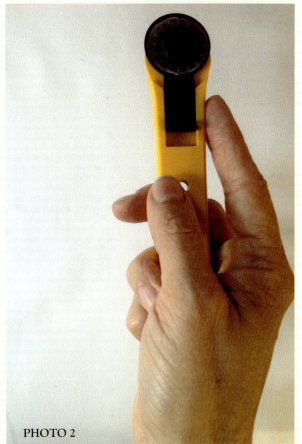

PHOTO 2

The blade angle is extremely important. Do not lean the blade in or out but keep a 90 degree angle with the template and the mat. (Photo 3)

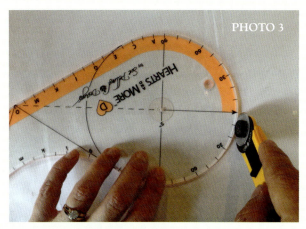
PHOTO 3

NON-SLIP GRIPS

Slipping on fabrics can be a nuisance when cutting with Hearts and More or any template or ruler. I have found a wonderful product that virtually eliminates slipping. Grace TrueGrips are thin rubber disks that attach firmly to the back of your rulers and templates. Unlike sandpaper dots that tend to fall off and leave a sticky

residue, the Grace TrueGrips will not fall off. Grace TrueGrips are clear so they will not hinder your view of the template markings or the fabric and board under your tool.

Two or three TrueGrips are used down the center of standard rulers, but for Hearts and More only one grip is needed on each end of the template. Place the donut shaped grip over the hole in the center of each circle on each end of the tool. You will still be able to access the hole in the tool for marking or pinning through. I put TrueGrips on both sides of the Hearts and More templates. When using the tools, it is nice to be able to turn the tool over and cut with either the front or back side facing up.

Grace TrueGrips come with fifteen large grips to a package. The grips look like donuts and you will find there are also 15 "donut holes". Use the donut holes on the smaller sized templates.

One package will cover all four templates on both the front and back sides. You will have additional grip material in the package that can be cut and used on other rulers in your work room. They are a great value.

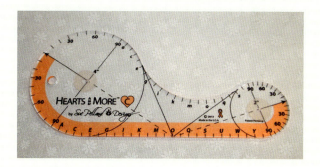

CUTTING MATS

Be sure to have a good cutting mat to use with your templates. If your board is old and no longer pliable you may need to replace it. After much use and over time your board can lose its elasticity. Instead of your blade sinking into the board with every cut, your blade rides on top of your board and you may not get a clean cut. A new, soft, self-healing mat may solve the problem.

A standard cutting mat will be sufficient for cutting with Hearts and More. If you use a standard mat, you will need to place the mat on the corner of your table. Place it on the right corner of the table if you are right-handed and the left corner of the table if you are left-handed. Walk around the corner of the table as you cut. Try each cut on paper first to learn the best way to position the fabric, the tool, and the mat for cutting.

ROTATING CUTTING MATS

Whether you are right-handed or left-handed, you can hold the fabric and the tool in the same way as is pictured in the instructions of this book. When you start cutting begin at the point that feels right for you. For example, a left-handed person will start a straight-edge heart at the top and a right-handed person will start the cut at the bottom of the heart.

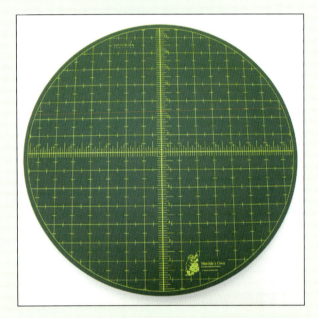

Using a rotating mat greatly helps left and right-handed people as you can move the board around to find the safest and easiest position to start cutting. As you cut, you will always push the rotary cutter away from your body. As soon as your hand position starts to get uncomfortable, rotate the mat as needed to keep the rotary blade moving in a forward motion.

Reposition your tool holding hand as needed to keep your position natural and not awkward. We want our fingers to stay safe and cutting at an awkward angle is not safe.

Some rotating mats are easier to use than others. Two brands that I recommend are the Matilda and the Martelli rotating mat. These two mats rotate on ball bearings giving you complete control over the rotation with very little effort. With downward pressure, the rotating mat remains still for cutting. Relieve the pressure and you can rotate the mat freely to a more comfortable position. Either of these mats allows you to do this while cutting without lifting your blade.

The Martelli mat has wonderful markings, especially the 60 degree marking for folding flowers. (Chapter 4) The Martelli also has a replaceable cutting mat and an optional pressing surface that can be used with the rotating mat. If you wear out the cutting surface, you can replace this piece without replacing the rotating base.

My favorite rotating mat is the Matilda mat. Its self-healing green cutting surface is permanently attached to the rotating base. I like the simplicity of the one piece construction and I like that the mat is supported by the base all the way to the edges. I do not recommend a square rotating mat as they are difficult to turn while cutting.

PRACTICE MAKES PERFECT!

While you are learning, it is more economical to start practicing with paper rather than fabric. Learn to cut each of the shapes and practice the most comfortable cutting position for each shape. Once you have mastered each shape with paper then start working with fabric. Paper is easier to cut than fabric so continue practicing with unfused scrap fabric to ensure that you can get clean cuts around the curves.

Troubleshooting when Cutting

If you get a rough edge:

1) Cut fewer layers. Start with shapes cut with one fold before you graduate to shapes cut with two folds. This will mean cutting two layers instead of four until you are confident.
2) Take your time cutting. Try cutting about ½" at a time. Don't rush!
3) Make sure the fusible side of your fabric is completely cool and folded in so the fusible sides are together when folded. Sometimes cutting fusible side up makes the fusible stick to the blade.
4) Make sure you have grips on the under side of your template to prevent your tools from slipping.
5) Put a new blade in your rotary cutter or try a different brand of cutter if you have one.
6) Review the angle of your blade. It needs to be perpendicular to your mat and straight along the edge of your template. (Photo 3 on page 13)
7) Try a different cutting mat.

A few more tools that will make your life easier

QUILTER'S CHALK LINE

Another tool I developed is the Quilter's Chalk Line. The Quilter's Chalk Line is based on a carpenter's chalk line and is used to make straight, accurate, removable lines on quilts or fabrics.

The tool has a 30-foot cotton line inside a hollow plastic casing. The plastic casing has a rubber door on it where you can add powdered chalk. The line winds up inside the case and as you pull it out a thin layer of chalk coats the line. By stretching the line tight and giving it a snap you can make a straight line between any two points. In my chalk line, I use iron-erasable chalk powder because I am often marking backgrounds for fusible appliqué. Fusing the appliqué with a hot iron removes the guidelines.

The Quilter's Chalk Line is the most efficient and accurate method of marking a grid for your appliqué backgrounds.

The Quilter's Chalk Line is a valuable tool when you need to square up your quilts prior to binding. You want four straight sides and four 90 degree corners on your quilts to help them hang or lay flat. By using your Quilter's Chalk Line and a large square template you can easily mark four square, straight sides on your quilts. If a mistake is made when marking your quilt, the chalk rubs or irons off so you can mark your edges perfectly before cutting. Marking with the chalk line prior to cutting eliminates errors in cutting. You will never cut off something important or cut crooked sides again!

One final way to use your Quilter's Chalk Line is for marking any straight line quilting designs such as cross hatching. There is no need to iron your quilt as the chalk rubs off with a microfiber cloth.

PATTERN CUTTING BOARD

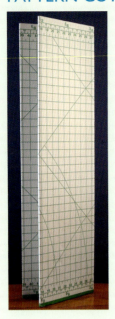

Pattern cutting boards make marking grids even easier when used with the Quilter's Chalk Line. This cardboard mat is marked in 1" increments. Place your fabric over the printed grid so that you can see the markings on each edge. Use a T-pin to hold one end of your chalk line. Stretch the chalk line taut between parallel markings and snap. You will get nice straight lines on your fabric at exact increments.

Additional Marking Products

BOHIN MECHANICAL CHALK MARKING PENCIL

This tool makes a very thin line that will not wear off before you want it to. The chalk colors can be changed but I keep this one for my favorite white chalk. I use this when marking hand or machine quilting designs on darker fabrics.

HERA MARKER

This tool is used to mark along the edges of the templates. Held like a rotary cutter, this tool leaves a shiny line or crease as you press it into the fabric. Primarily I use this for hand quilting designs marked with the template as the lines are a little more difficult to see when machine quilting. No removal is necessary and it works on all colors of fabric, even white.

CHALK WHEEL

There are a few different brands of chalk wheels such as the blue and red ones shown at left. This tool is primarily used for marking quilting designs. I find it very helpful when marking placement of vines and serpentine edges as well. It can be used as is from the package or you can throw away the chalk inside and replace it with iron-erase chalk.

IRON-ERASE CHALK POWDER BY SUE PELLAND DESIGNS

This handy resealable bottle of chalk has a dispenser top to easily fill your chalk line and other chalk marking tools. The heat sensitive chalk evaporates when in contact with a hot iron (with or without steam). It also brushes away with a microfiber cloth.

PILOT FRIXION PEN

This iron-away pen comes in many different colors. I prefer to use chalk whenever I can, but on white quilts I use dots made with Frixion pens to mark the corners of my grids. Most of the time the appliqué will cover the dots, but if not, the markings go away with a hot iron. Warning: The markings will come back if you put your quilt in the freezer (or store your quilts in a cold attic!) Use a hot hair dryer to remove the lines if they recur.

I am very cautious when using the Frixion marking pen. This pen was not intended for fabric, and the fact that the lines may come back in cold temperatures means that the pen is leaving chemicals on your fabric. No one knows the long term effects of these chemicals so use this pen sparingly and only where the markings will be covered with appliqué. I would never use this pen for marking quilting designs.

CHAPTER 3:
Master the Cutting Techniques
Cutting with One Fold

The following shapes are cut by folding your fabric and placing the Hearts and More template in different positions on the fold: Circles, Leaves, Straight-edge Teardrops, Curved-edge Teardrops, Straight-edge Hearts, and Curved-edge Hearts.

Experimentation is the best way to find the shape you want to make. Sue Pelland Designs patterns will give you the outline of the shapes for each project and will also give measurements from the templates to show you exactly how to reproduce the shapes. The best way to learn each shape is to cut the shapes from a folded piece of paper. Using paper will eliminate waste while you learn the variations in each shape. Working with paper also gives you a "dry run" to figure out the most comfortable cutting position on your flat or rotating mat.

Follow the step by step instructions for each shape. Rotate your mat or walk around your stationary mat to find the most comfortable position for cutting. Left-handed people will find cutting tips in the box on page 26.

It does not matter if you start cutting at the bottom or top of each shape. This will change depending on whether you are using the small or the large end of the template. Likewise, keeping the fold on the right or the left will depend on which end of the template you are using, and if you are comfortable reading the template from the wrong side.

Even in the step by step instructions, you may find that the template is flipped so the numbers and letters are backwards. Just flip your template to match the photo in the instructions.

SPD305 Conversation Hearts. Made by Sue Pelland and Susan Arena, Quilted by Shirley Tetreault

SHAPE 1: CIRCLE

There are two circle sizes on each of the four Hearts and More templates. Circles are a great addition to your rotary cut appliqué shapes and can be easily cut on the fold of your fabric.

Circles range from 1" to 5" across (diameter) depending on which template you use. The only circle that I do not cut with the rotary cutter is the 1" circle. All shapes cut with the 1" side of Template A are too small to cut with a rotary cutter. Cut these shapes by folding the fabric, marking around the 1" circle with a Frixion pen, then cut on the inside of the marked line with sharp scissors. Keep the fabric folded and pinch as close to the line as you can with your fingers while you cut around the circle.

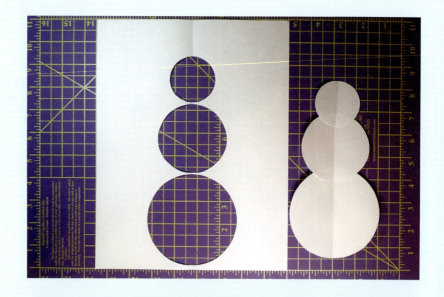

Blue Moons. Made by Nancy Sullivan, Quilted by Kathryn Amadon

Cut a Circle: Step by Step

STEP 1: Fold the fabric. Make sure your fold is at least half the width of the circle you want to cut.

STEP 2: Place the 90 degree markings and the straight line on the fold of your fused fabric. (Photo 1)

STEP 3: Cut with a 28mm rotary cutter and a sharp blade. Keep the blade down and rotate the mat as needed to cut a half circle.

STEP 4: Offset a second row of circles for the most efficient use of fabric. (Photos 2 and 3)

ALTERNATE METHOD: Multiple layers of fabric can also be cut into a circle by placing the template on a stack of squares and cutting at least half way around the circle. (Photo 4)

Rotate the tool to place the solid circle line over the cut edge that you just cut. Continue cutting around the circle to make up to four circles at one time. (Photo 5)

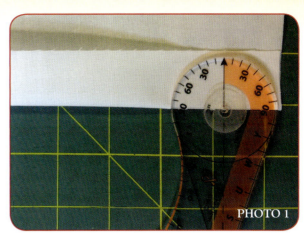
PHOTO 1

PHOTO 2

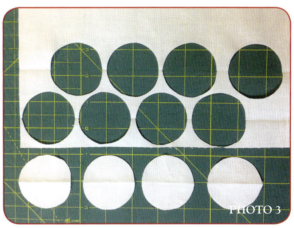
PHOTO 3

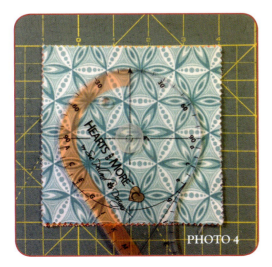
PHOTO 4

PHOTO 5

SHAPE 2: SIMPLE LEAF OR MELON

Simple leaves or melons are the most common shapes in appliqué quilts. This is the perfect leaf or petal shape for so many appliqué projects. Entire quilts can be built around this one shape. The best tool to make leaf shapes fast is the Leaves Galore template also by Sue Pelland Designs. With this tool you can make dozens of leaves at one time by stacking four layers of fabric and making multiple leaves with every cut.

The benefit to using the Hearts and More tool is that you can cut a wider variety of the leaf shapes and sizes. Simple leaves can be cut using the round ends of the Hearts and More template. Cut symmetrical leaves by folding fabric. Cut leaves of varying widths, the largest being 60 to 60 degrees, and the smallest being around 30 to 30 degrees. (Photo 6)

Adjust the sizes in between by choosing two degree markings. The two markings do not have to have the same label, for example, you can cut a leaf from 50 to 40 degrees that is between 50 to 50 degrees and 40 to 40 degrees. This gives you seven different sized leaves on each end of the four templates for a total of 56 leaf sizes. Some are short and fat while others are long and slim.

Enough Love to Go Around. Made by Sue Pelland, Quilted by Kathy Sperino

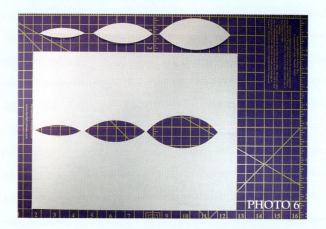

Hearts and Leaves block. Made by Linda Gosselin

Cut a Simple Leaf or Melon Shape: Step by Step

STEP 1: Fold the fabric. Make sure your fold is at least half the width of the leaf you want to cut.

STEP 2: Place the Hearts and More template with the end of the template over the fold. Place two tic marks on the fold such as the two 50 degree markings, one on the orange side and one on the clear side. (Photo 7)

STEP 3: Move the template to a higher number to make a longer fatter leaf. Move the template to a smaller number to get a thinner, shorter leaf.

STEP 4: Cut using a 28mm rotary cutter. Unfold and check the size.

STEP 5: Continue down the fold to make as many leaves as you need for the project. (Photo 8)

STEP 6: Offset the second row of leaves to utilize the fabric in the best way possible. (Photos 9 and 10)

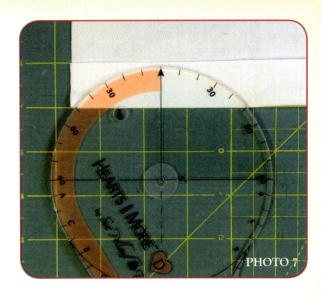

PHOTO 7

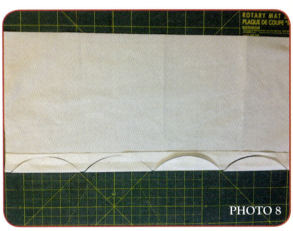

PHOTO 8

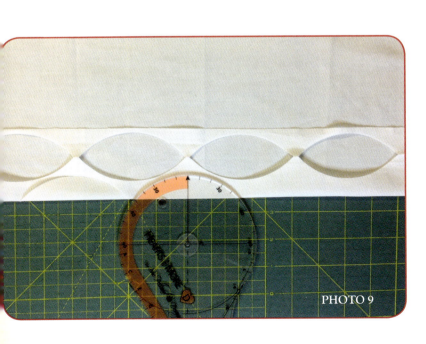

PHOTO 9

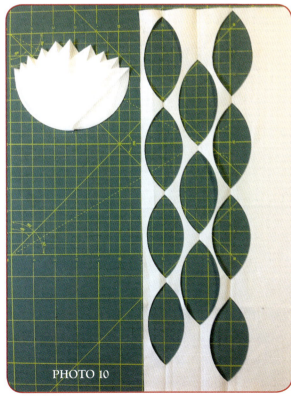

PHOTO 10

SHAPE 3: STRAIGHT-EDGE TEARDROP OR FLOWER PETAL

Flower petals with straight sides and a rounded end are cut with the Hearts and More template. Use the dashed line that ends in an arrow at the zero degree marking on each end of the template. Two straight-edge teardrop shapes are outlined on each template. However, many sizes and shapes of teardrops can be made. Vary the length and the width of the teardrop by angling the template on the fold to end at any capital letter on the straight side of the template. See the chart in the Appendix for the maximum width and length of teardrops that can be made with each end of the tool.

Cut a Straight-Edge Teardrop or Flower Petal: Step by Step

STEP 1: Make sure the folded fabric is at least half the width of the teardrop you want to cut.

STEP 2: Place the Hearts and More template with the dashed line on the fold. (Photo 11)

STEP 3: Cut using a 28mm rotary cutter. Unfold and check the size. (Photo 13)

STEP 4: Continue down the fold to make as many teardrops as you need for the project. (Photo 12)

STEP 5: Offset the second row of teardrops to utilize the fabric in the best way possible. (Photo 13)

STEP 6: Move the template onto a different end point to make your straight-edge teardrop longer or shorter. You may also adjust your starting point to keep the shape round on the top. In this example, we started at 10 degrees instead of Zero. (Photo 14)

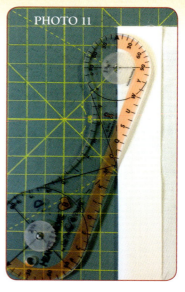
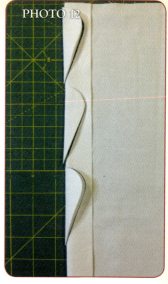

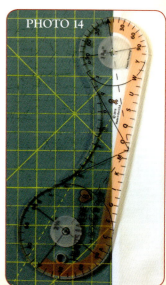

SHAPE 4: CURVED-EDGE TEARDROPS (WATER DROPLETS)

Using either end of the template, make water droplet shapes using the curved-edge of the template. These shapes are perfect for raindrops, flower petals, and leaves. This is the first shape that does not have a straight line marking on the template to get you started.

Variations in the size of the water droplet are less numerous than the straight sided shapes.

Please refer to the chart in the Appendix for the range of sizes you can make with each tool. Water droplets can be made slightly wider by moving to the 20 degree or 30 degree marking on the orange side. Narrower water droplets can be made by moving to between Zero and 30 degrees on the clear side. Move the template to a different small letter on the curved side of the tool to make your water droplet longer or shorter.

Cut Curved Edge Teardrops (Water Droplets): Step by Step

STEP 1: Fold the fabric. Make sure the folded fabric is at least half the width of the water droplet.

STEP 2: Place the Hearts and More tool with the 10 degree marking (orange side) and the small letter "o" on the fold. (Photo 15)

STEP 3: Cut using a 28mm rotary cutter. Unfold and check the size. (Photo 16)

STEP 4: Continue down the fold to make as many shapes as you need for the project.

STEP 5: Offset the second row of water droplets to utilize the fabric in the best way possible. (Photo 17)

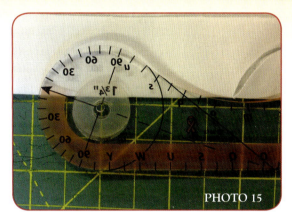
PHOTO 15

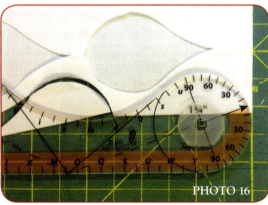
PHOTO 16

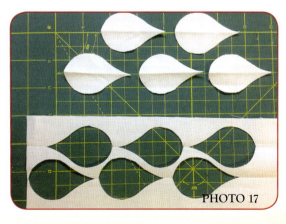
PHOTO 17

SHAPE 5: STRAIGHT-EDGE HEARTS

There are two straight-edge heart shapes marked on each of the Hearts and More templates. Look for the lines that make the ice cream cone shape on each end of the template.

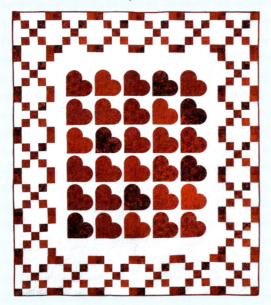

SPD305 Conversation Hearts. Made by Sue Pelland and Donna Hopkins, Quilted by Shirley Tetreault

Straight-edge hearts in the step by step instructions are made by placing this straight line on the fold of the fabric. You can lengthen or shorten the heart shape by adjusting the template to different angles. (Photos 18 and 19)

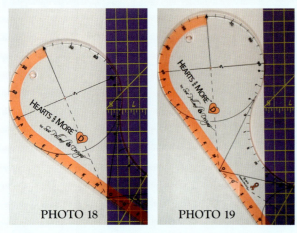

While the inside "V" is normally made by placing the 90 degree marking on the fold, the starting point and ending point are both variable. Experiment on paper with the bottom of the heart ending on different capital letters on the orange side of the template. See the chart in the Appendix for size variations of the straight-edge hearts.

Generally, the starting position for the inside "V" at the top of the heart is the 90 degree marking. However, for a "V" that is more shallow, try 70 or 80 degrees. Anything less than 70 degrees does not work well for a fusible heart shape.

If you choose to hand appliqué a heart shape, you will want the top of the heart to start at 60 degrees. While 60 degrees makes a "V" that is too shallow for fusible appliqué, it is perfect for hand appliqué. Once you clip straight down into the "V" and turn under a scant ¼", your finished heart will have a pleasing shape.

When cutting straight-edge hearts out of a square, it is useful to fold the square on the diagonal. The straight-edge heart will fit nicely into one corner of the square. (Photo 20) The remainder of the square can be used for a smaller heart, circle, or other single fold shape. Photo 20 shows the bonus hearts being cut for the Conversation Hearts Mini quilt made from the leftover fabrics from the larger quilt. The bonus miniature quilt is a free pattern on our website. Watch the video on YouTube that shows how to stencil the hearts.

Conversation Hearts Mini: Free bonus pattern available online at suepellanddesigns.com

Cut Straight-Edge Hearts: Step by Step

STEP 1: Fold the fabric. Make sure the folded fabric is at least half the width of the straight-edge heart you want to cut.

STEP 2: Place the Hearts and More tool with the 90 degree marking (clear side) and the capital letter "N" on the fold. (Photo 21)

STEP 3: Cut using a 28mm rotary cutter. Unfold and check the size.

STEP 4: Continue down the fold to make as many straight-edge hearts as you need for the project. (Photo 22)

STEP 5: Offset the second row of straight-edge hearts to utilize the fabric in the best way possible. (Photo 23)

PHOTO 21

PHOTO 22

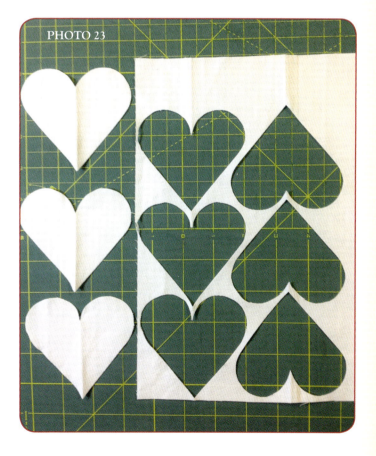
PHOTO 23

SHAPE 6: CURVED-EDGE HEARTS

Using either the small side or the large side of the template, make curved-edge hearts by placing the curved edge on your cutting side. Both left-handed and right-handed people will place the fold on your right and will select two markings on the template to place on the fold. Like the water droplets, this shape does not have a straight line marking on the tool to get you started. To learn to make the curved-edge heart, use the step by step instructions.

Variations in the size of the curved-edge heart are less numerous than the straight sided hearts. I do not recommend using anything but the 90 degree marking at the top of your heart. Move the ending point to a different small letter on the curved side of the tool to make your heart slightly longer or shorter. Please refer to the chart in the Appendix for the range of sizes you can make with each template.

SPD303 Bouquet. Made by Sue Pelland and Joanne Bertrand, Quilted by Linda Gosselin

> There are some variations between the heart on the right and the heart on the left. The heart on the left has a deeper indent on the top of the heart and a longer bottom point. The heart on the right has a shallower indent and a shorter bottom point.

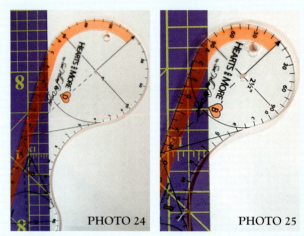

PHOTO 24   PHOTO 25

Elongated curved-edge heart   Short curved-edge heart

Cutting with Hearts and More Templates for Left-Handed Quilters

Left-handed quilters will set up their cutting board, fabric, and template exactly the same as right-handed quilters. Rotate the board until you find a comfortable place to start cutting. Usually, left-handers start cutting in the top left, rotating the mat counterclockwise.

For example, when cutting the heart, left-handers will have the fold on the left, and the curved edge of the template on the right. Left-handers will start cutting at the top indent of the heart and rotate counterclockwise to the bottom point.

Right-handed quilters will have the fold on the left, and the curved edge of the template on the right. Right-handers will start cutting at the bottom point, then rotate the mat clockwise to continue cutting around the half circle then end at the top of the heart.

Cut Curved-Edge Hearts: Step by Step

STEP 1: Fold the fabric. Make sure the folded fabric is at least half the width of the curved-edge heart you want to make.

STEP 2: Place the Hearts and More template with the 0 degree marking (orange side) and the lower case letter "m" on the fold. (Photo 26)

STEP 3: Cut using a 28mm rotary cutter. Unfold and check the size.

STEP 4: Continue down the fold to make as many curved-edge hearts as you need for the project. (Photo 27)

STEP 5: Turn the fabric so that when you fold you can see the previously cut hearts. Now fit the template into the space between two hearts. (Photo 27) Offset the second row of hearts to utilize the fabric in the most efficient way possible. (Photo 28)

PHOTO 26

PHOTO 27

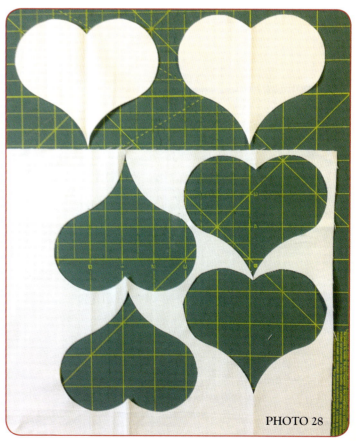
PHOTO 28

27

CHAPTER 4: More Cutting Techniques

CUTTING WITH MULTIPLE FOLDS AND/OR MULTIPLE CUTS

A few more useful shapes can be cut by folding your fabric more than once and placing the Hearts and More template in different positions on the folds: ovals, four petal flowers, six petal flowers, and eight petal flowers.

Follow the step by step instructions to learn the technique for each shape. Once again, the best way to learn each shape is to cut them out from a folded piece of paper. Using paper will eliminate fabric waste while you learn the variations of each shape. Working with paper also gives you a "dry run" to figure out the most comfortable cutting position on your flat or rotating mat. Move your paper, your tools, and your mat to find the most comfortable position to start cutting. You should always cut away from yourself. Rotate the mat as the shape turns so you continue to cut away from your body.

Sue Pelland Designs patterns will give you the outline of each shape for each project as well as give measurements from the templates to show you exactly how to reproduce each shape.

SHAPE 7: OVAL

There are many oval sizes that can be made from each end of the Hearts and More tools. Ovals range in size from less than 2" long to 21" long depending on which template you use. The only ovals that I do not cut with the rotary cutter are those made with the 1" circle. Cut these shapes by folding the fabric, marking around the 1" circle with a Frixion pen, then cut on the inside of the marked line with sharp scissors.

SPD301 Unchain My Heart. Made by Sue Pelland, Quilted by Shirley Tetreault

There is a limit to the width of the finished oval. Check the chart in the Appendix to ensure that your desired oval is possible using the Hearts and More tools. Use the straight (orange) side of the template and the curved end to make the oval shape. You can make the oval as long or as short as you like depending on where you place the curved end. The best oval shape is made by using the 30 degree mark on the orange side of the tool on the left hand fold of the fabric. You can use any mark to the right of the 30 degree mark, but you may start to get a pointy oval instead of one with a nice rounded end. Make sure you experiment on paper first.

Cut Ovals: Step by Step

STEP 1: Determine the size of the finished oval. Cut a rectangle of fused fabric slightly larger than the finished oval size. See the chart in the Appendix for finished sizes.

STEP 2: Fold your fabric in half across the length then in half again across the width. (Photo 1)

STEP 3: Place the folded fabric on a cutting mat with the folded edges on the left and bottom; line up with horizontal and vertical lines on the mat. (Photo 1)

STEP 4: Place the template with the straight side parallel to the vertical lines on the mat and parallel to the raw edges of the fabric. Adjust the template to get the correct width and height for the oval. (Photo 2) Use a secondary ruler if needed to keep the right edge of the template square to the edge of the fabric.

STEP 5: Cut with a 28mm rotary cutter with a sharp blade, keeping blade down and rotating mat as needed to cut one quarter of the oval. (Photo 3)

STEP 6: Unfold and check oval for size. (Photo 4)

PHOTO 1

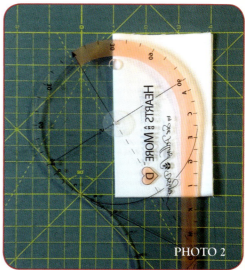

PHOTO 2

PHOTO 3

PHOTO 4

SHAPE 8: FOUR PETAL FLOWERS OR CLOVER LEAF SHAPES

Several different flowers can be made with the round end of the Hearts and More tools. By folding the fabric in fourths, sixths, or eighths you can make four petal, six petal, or eight petal flowers. Flowers can be cut from circles or squares of fused fabric. Cutting from oversized squares results in a bonus frame. See the box below for more information about frames.

Cutting Shapes from Oversized Squares

Using oversized squares is useful when cutting each of the shapes if your project requires a positive and a negative block. Even if you will not be using the negative block for the current project, consider cutting circles, ovals, hearts, flowers and more shapes out of oversized fused fabric squares.

As long as the original square is at least 1" larger than the size of your finished circle, heart, etc., the resulting frame can be used in the same quilt or in another bonus quilt. In the "Play Ball" version of SPD306: Spin Me 'Round, two-toned circles are cut from a half-square triangle block. The resulting half-square triangle has a negative space where the circle was cut out. By placing the half-square triangle over a stitched white fabric, the baseballs form a reverse appliqué block. The two-toned circles are "bonus pieces" that were used to finish the border of this quilt. The Blue Moons Quilt in the Project Section is another practical use of this technique.

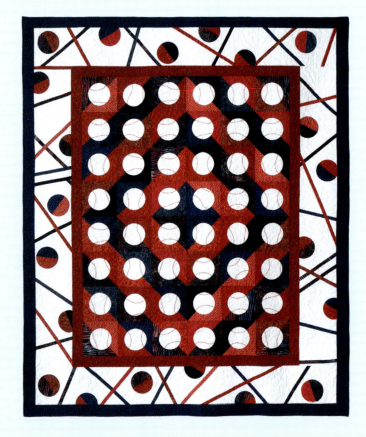

Cut Four Petal Flowers: Step by Step

STEP 1: Determine the size of the finished flower. Cut a square of fused fabric slightly larger than the finished flower size. See the chart in the Appendix for standard sizes.

STEP 2: Fold your fabric in half across the length then in half again across the width. (Photo 5)

STEP 3: Place the folded fabric on a cutting mat with the folded edges on the left and bottom; line up with horizontal and vertical lines on the mat. The center of the square is the point on the bottom left of the folded square. (Photo 5)

STEP 4: Place the template with the same two numbers on the two folds and the dashed line ending in an arrow through the center of the square. Adjust the template to make sure all three points are matching. (Photo 6)

STEP 5: Cut with a 28mm rotary cutter with a sharp blade, keeping blade down and rotating mat as needed to cut from fold to fold. Use the flower and the frame if desired. (Photo 7)

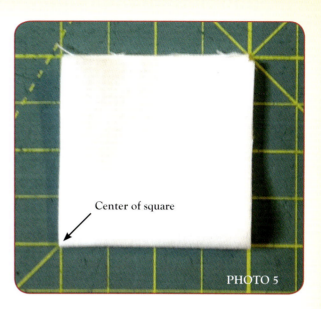

PHOTO 5

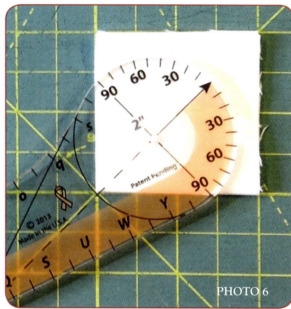

PHOTO 6

PHOTO 7

31

SHAPE 9: SIX & EIGHT PETAL FLOWERS

As long as I can remember I have been using six petal flowers in my quilts. Making templates out of template plastic when there were only a few shapes to cut was tedious, yet I felt it was the best way to get accurately cut flowers. Now that I have Hearts and More, six petal flowers are simple once you learn how to fold your fabric correctly. After accurately folding your fabric, the best way to cut six petal flowers is to mark the half circle with a Frixion pen and cut through the six layers with scissors. Cut on the inside of the marked line. Any ink remaining will iron away when you fuse your six petal flower. Once again, you can utilize the square from which you cut your six petal flower as well as the flower itself.

A chart showing the variations in possible flower sizes can be found in the Appendix. Please refer to the step by step instructions on the next page.

Eight petal flowers are made in a similar way. Fold the square in quarters, then fold back each quarter into a triangle. This will form an accordion style fold in eighths. (Photo 8) Staple if desired to keep folds crisp. Mark with an appropriate marking tool from 90 to 90 degrees (Photo 9), and cut with scissors. (Photo 10 and 11)

For all four, six, and eight petal flowers, the two markings that you place on the folds can be adjusted for deep or shallow indentations between petals. Always keep the dashed line ending with the arrow centered on the triangle and running through the center of the square.

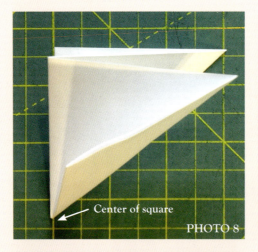

PHOTO 8

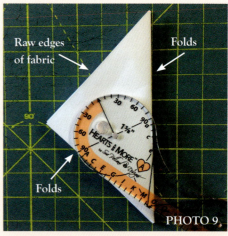

PHOTO 9

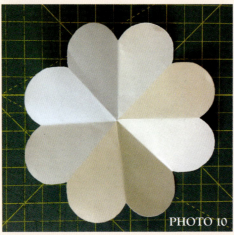

PHOTO 10

PHOTO 11

Cut Six Petal Flowers: Step by Step

STEP 1: Determine the size of the finished flower. Cut a square of fused fabric slightly larger than the finished flower size. See the chart in the Appendix for standard sizes.

STEP 2: Fold your fabric in half across the length then in half again across the width to find the center of your square. Finger press both folds.

STEP 3: Locate a 60 degree angle line on your cutting mat. If your mat does not have a 60 degree line, use a ruler with a 60 degree line.

STEP 4: Unfold the fabric one time and place the center of the square at a point where the 60 degree line crosses a horizontal line on your mat. (Photo 12)

STEP 5: Place a straight edge along the 60 degree angle line. Fold the right side of the fabric up so the fold meets the straight edge. This creates fold two. (Photo 13)

STEP 6: Pick up the folded fabric lightly pinching fold two. Fold the fabric to the left of the center point under so fold one is lined up with fold three to make an accordion fold. Staple if desired as indicated. (Photo 14)

STEP 7: Place the template with two matching numbers on the two folds, and the dashed line ending in an arrow through the center of the fabric. Adjust the template to make sure all three points are matching. (Photo 15)

STEP 8: Mark the half circle with a Frixion pen. Pick up the marked and folded fabric making sure all layers remain lined up and folds remain crisp. Pinch close to the marked line and cut on the inside of the marked line with scissors. (Photo 16)

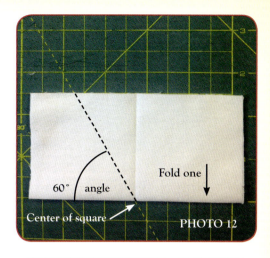

PHOTO 12

PHOTO 13

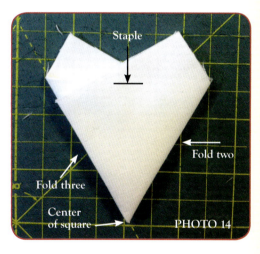

PHOTO 14

PHOTO 15

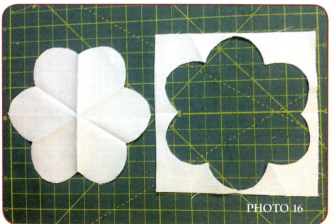

PHOTO 16

Making Multiple Cuts

RINGS AND CHAINS

There are times when I want to alter a shape by making multiple cuts. Rings are one example of a shape made with multiple cuts. Rings can be made with any shape and in a variety of sizes. The goal is to find two template ends that work together to make your rings. In this example, use the 5" circle on Template D to cut 5" circles from fused fabric. (Photo 17) Next, center a 4" circle (Template C) inside the 5" circle. Cut to make a ring. (Photo 18)

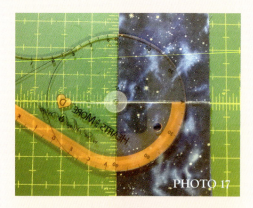

The square frame and the 4" circle make the Blue Moons quilt on page 60. The bonus rings give you a starting point for another project or use them to jazz up the back of the Blue Moons Quilt. (Photo 19)

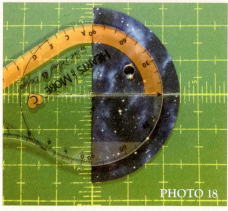

Once you learn to make a ring, making a chain from those rings is simple. The rings become the links in the chain by cutting one link where it crosses another. Tuck the cut ends under the previous link and you have a chain. (Photos 20, 21, and 22) Try the heart shaped chain in the Row Quilt (page 86) to practice making chains. Unchain My Heart (page 28) uses oval links for chains. Bouquet uses curved-edge heart links.

SPD304 Bouquet. Made by Sue Pelland

Quilts using large heart rings include "He Loves Me" and "Jasmine". After assembling the large flower blocks using the frame and a small flower there are seventeen flower rings remaining as a bonus. Use these flower rings for the beginning of a second quilt or incorporate them into the quilt back.

SPD303 He Loves Me. Made by Sue Pelland, Quilted by Shirley Tetreault

SPD302 Jasmine. Made by Sue Pelland

Quilt block

Bonus block

Additional appliqué shapes can be achieved by using the templates in some unconventional ways. Use the templates to round the corners of geometric shapes such as squares, rectangles, and triangles. Using the templates to alter shapes cut with Leaves Galore templates makes more interesting appliqué shapes.

After cutting leaves with Leaves Galore four layers at a time, each stack of four leaves can be modified by rounding with the appropriate size circle from the Hearts and More templates. (Photo 23) Photo 24 shows all six leaf sizes made with the Leaves Galore full set, then trimmed with the appropriate Hearts and More tool to round one end. A chart that indicates which Hearts and More template size is used with each leaf size can be found in the Appendix.

PHOTO 23

PHOTO 24

CHAPTER 5: Special Quilts

When looking at curved pieced quilts, think carefully about how the curves could be adapted for appliqué rather than curved piecing. In this chapter we will show you Hearts and More techniques that simplify these complex patterns and achieve the desired look without the difficulty of curved piecing. Yoyo quilts are another special technique that can be cut quickly and accurately with the Hearts and More tools. These two antique quilts found at Quilt Market in Houston are examples of quilts that could be made with Hearts and More techniques.

Method One: Clam Shells Made with Hand Appliqué

Layer up to four layers of freezer paper, shiny side up. Cut the four layers of freezer paper into 5" squares. Tack the four squares together in the corners with an iron. Place the Hearts and More template on the freezer paper square centering the 5" circle on the square with the cross lines perpendicular to the straight edges of the paper. Cut the top half circle with a rotary cutter on a rotating mat. Move the template to the bottom left hand corner and place the quarter circle line along the two edges of the paper. Cut a quarter of a circle from the left corner. Repeat with the right corner. This is the finished size of the clam shell.

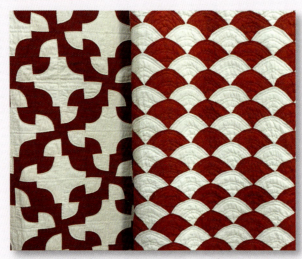

Antique Quilts from Cindy's Antique Quilts. For info on purchasing these quilts, contact Cindy or Ronnie Rennels at www.cindysantiquequilts.com

CLAM SHELL

Traditionally, Clam Shell quilts are made with turned edge appliqué, English Paper Piecing, or curved piecing. All three methods are labor intensive but create beautiful one patch quilts. The Hearts and More templates and rotary cutting speed up all three methods of making clam shells.

Traditional Clam Shell Quilt. Designed and Made by Donna Bozeman

Fuse the shiny side of the freezer paper pattern to the wrong side of a 5½" square of fabric. Trim the 5½" square approximately ¼" larger around all sides of the paper template. Use a small paint brush and apply a starch solution on the top rounded seam allowance. Using a hot iron and a wooden skewer, press the seam allowance over the freezer paper pattern making small pleats to create a smooth rounded edge on the top edge. Only prepare the top round edge of each clam shell. The bottom edges will be covered when you overlap the clam shells. Prepare all clam shells in this manner.

On a cutting mat or gridded pattern cutting board, lay out two clam shells side by side keeping each clam shell in a 5" square. Lay a third clam shell centered on the intersection between the first two, overlapping ¼" on the bottom edges matching the paper pattern with the finished top edge of each curve. Hand baste the prepared top edge to the seam allowance of the two clam shells above the one you are adding. Continue to build up your first two clam shell rows from right to left. Hand appliqué the top edge of row two to the seam allowance of row one. Continue adding rows, first hand basting, then completing with hand appliqué.

Clam Shell Table Topper. Designed and Made by Donna Bozeman

Method Two: English Paper Piecing

If you love English Paper Piecing, you can prepare the papers for this method using the Hearts and More templates. Without going into detail on how to complete a quilt with English Paper Piecing, I will get you started by teaching you to cut accurate clam shells from paper.

To make the papers for a 5" English Pieced clam shell, start with 5" squares of paper, and 5½" squares of fabric. To cut accurate clam shells from the paper, staple four layers of 5" squares together in the center of the square. Place the Hearts and More template on the paper squares centering the circle with the square with the cross lines perpendicular to the straight edges of the paper. Cut the top half circle with a rotary cutter on a rotating mat. Move the template to the bottom left hand corner and place the quarter circle line along the two edges of the paper. Cut a quarter of a circle from the left corner. Repeat with the right corner.

Table Runner. Designed and Made by Donna Bozeman

Place the paper on a 5½" square of fabric and trim the fabric to be ¼" larger than the paper. Hand turn and baste the seam allowances to the paper. Stitch edge to edge with a whip stitch or ladder stitch or use your favorite English Paper Piecing method to complete the clam shell quilt.

Method Three: Fusible Appliqué

You will need two types of clam shells for fusible appliqué. Clam shells with ¼" seam allowance on the lower edge and clam shells without seam allowance.

Clam shells without seam allowances are used on the bottom row of the clam shell border of the Kaffe Clam Shell project on page 53 and in the Table Topper on the left.

Clam Shells with No Seam Allowance: Step by Step

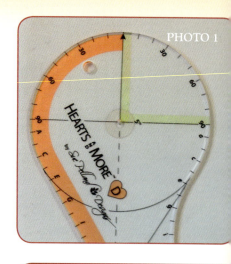

PHOTO 1

STEP 1: Mark the Hearts and More template with Glo-Line Tape or ¼" masking tape by placing the tape on the inside edge of the two straight lines crossing the 5" circle as shown. (Photo 1)

STEP 2: Prepare the fabric by fusing the back of the fabrics with Mistyfuse. Cut 5" squares of fused fabric. Layer four 5" squares with fusible side down on a rotating cutting mat. Line up the 5" square on straight lines on the board so that the center of the square is on a line in both directions.

STEP 3: Place the 5" end of Template D in the center of the 5" square matching lines on the board with the straight lines on the tool. Cut a half circle from the top of the square from 90 to 90 degrees. (Photo 2)

PHOTO 2

STEP 4: Place the 5" end of Template D so that the quarter circle marking is on the left and bottom edge of the left quarter square. Cut the full quarter circle. (Photo 3)

STEP 5: Repeat for the bottom right corner square (Photo 4) resulting in a clam shell with no seam allowance. (Photo 5)

Note: Make clam shells in any size from 1" to 5" using this method. Photo 6 shows five different sizes with no seam allowance.

PHOTO 3

PHOTO 4

PHOTO 5

PHOTO 6

Clam Shells with Seam Allowance: Step by Step

Most fusible clam shell quilts will require ¼" seam allowance on the two bottom corners. This is true for the top two rows of the clam shell border in the Kaffe quilt in the Project Section.

STEP 1,2,3: Follow instructions from previous page.

STEP 4: Place the 5" end of Template D so that the quarter circle marking is ¼" away from the left and bottom edge of the left quarter square. Use the Glo-Line Tape as your guide to cut ¼" less than a full quarter circle. Cut the corner as shown through all four layers. (Photo 7)

STEP 5: Repeat for the bottom right corner square. (Photo 8)
Photo 9 shows a clam shell with ¼" seam allowance on the bottom edge of the clam shell for fusible appliqué.

CLAM SHELL ASSEMBLY: When assembling rows of fusible clam shells, mark grid lines on your background fabric to help arrange the clam shells in straight rows. The distance between the grid lines is half the size of the finished clam shell. For example, when cutting a 5" clam shell, place grid lines at 2½" intervals. Lay the clam shells in straight rows, placing the edges and bottom of the first row of shells on the 5" lines. Fuse in place. Your second row of clam shells will rest on a line 2¼" below the first row, but you can't see this line once the first row is placed. Measure down 2¼" from the top edge of the first row and mark a line with iron-erase chalk. (Photo 10) Measure down 2½" for each subsequent row.

PHOTO 7

PHOTO 8

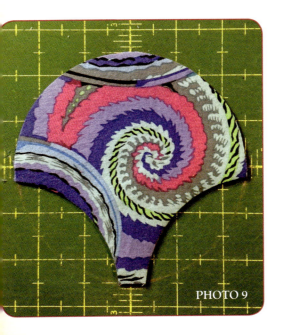
PHOTO 9

PHOTO 10

TILE QUILTS

While writing this book I took a wonderful trip with my husband to Spain. The influence of the Moors on Spanish architecture is evident everywhere especially in window openings and tile patterns. The shapes are similar to what you would expect to see in Morocco just across the Straight of Gibraltar from Spain's south coast. Quilts based on these architectural shapes are similar to the classic quilt pattern Gothic Windows and also resemble the quilt pattern Hearts and Gizzards. SPD Certified Instructor Donna Hopkins developed a fusible appliqué method that eliminates curved piecing and we call this type of quilt a Tile Quilt.

Gothic Windows Table Runner. Designed and Made by Donna Hopkins

Tiles Blocks: Step by Step

STEP 1: Cut two light squares of fabric.

STEP 2: Fuse the dark fabric and let it cool. Cut one dark square the same size as the light squares.

PHOTO 11

STEP 3: Fold the fused square in half on the diagonal. Place the Hearts and More tool on the raw edge of the triangle with the arrow along the straight edge. Keep the point of the triangle on the edge of the circle, and the 90 degree marking on the fold. (Photo 11) Repeat on the opposite corner. (Photo 12)

STEP 4: Place the center portion of the dark square on a light square, matching corners. Fuse in place. (Photo 13)

STEP 5: Place the two heart-shaped cutouts on two opposite corners of the second light square as shown. Fuse in place. (Photo 14)

STEP 6: Stitch raw edges of both squares with your favorite finishing method.

Note: Use any size square to start and find the most compatible Hearts and More tool to cut the corners of the square. Find instructions for two Tile Quilts in the Project Section on pages 66-72, a chart of whole number finished block sizes in the Appendix, or experiment to find the best size combination for your own Tile Quilt.

PHOTO 12

PHOTO 13

PHOTO 14

DRUNKARD'S PATH QUILTS

Drunkard's Path is traditionally a two-color, curved pieced block that many beginner and intermediate quilters shy away from. The curved piecing is hard to do on such small pieces of fabric making Drunkard's Path best suited for advanced quilters, until now.

We have an easy way to make Drunkard's Path blocks using the Hearts and More templates. Like most Sue Pelland Designs' quilts, our Drunkard's Path blocks are made with fusible appliqué instead of curved piecing.

There are dozens of Drunkard's Path variations that you can explore once you learn the basic Drunkard's Path technique.

For most Drunkard's Path variations, you will need equal numbers of light background and dark background blocks. Our method makes four light background squares and four dark background squares at once. These eight squares will make two of the Flying Bird blocks and two Diamond blocks. (Photos 15 and 16) Wall quilts featuring the flying birds variation and the diamond variation are found in the Project Section on page 76.

Photo 17 shows the four different Drunkard's Path block sizes made from the suggested block sizes in the Appendix. These four block sizes start with circles found on the large set of Hearts and More templates: 5", 4", 3" and 2". Finished block sizes are 3½", 2¾", 2" and 1¼".

The step by step instructions use the 5" circle to make a 3½" finished block.

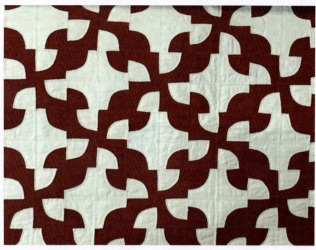

Antique Red and White Drunkard's Path Quilt, Winding Ways variation. Photo courtesy of Cindy's Antique Quilts

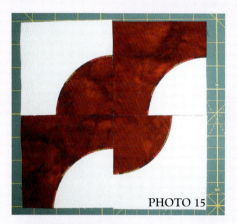

PHOTO 15

PHOTO 16

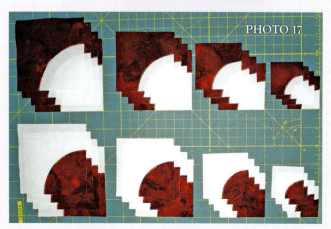

PHOTO 17

Drunkard's Path: Step by Step

STEP 1: Fuse the 6" square of Mistyfuse on the center of the dark 8¼" squares using an appliqué pressing sheet. Let cool for at least 15 minutes. (Photo 18)

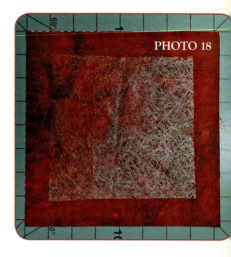

PHOTO 18

STEP 2: Fold the 8¼" squares along the diagonal in both directions and finger press. Keep the squares folded along one diagonal line. Place both diagonals on straight lines on your cutting mat.

STEP 3: Place the 5" end of Template D on the fold with the centering line on the fold and the arrow pointing at the top corner. (Photo 19)

STEP 4: Cut the 5" circle from the center of the 8¼" dark squares using a 28mm rotary cutter with a new, sharp blade. A clean cut is imperative because you will be using both the circle and the frame with the circle cut out. (Photo 20)

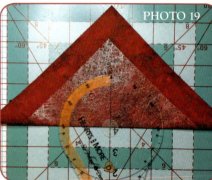

PHOTO 19

STEP 5: Place the frames right side down on an appliqué pressing sheet. Place the light 6" squares right side down to cover the 6" square of Mistyfuse on the back of the frame. Use a pressing sheet on top of the square to protect your iron. Press to fuse. (Photo 21)

STEP 6: Center the 5" dark circles on the 8¼" light background squares. Press to fuse. (Photo 21)

PHOTO 20

STEP 7: Complete decorative stitching around all circles.

STEP 8: Once the squares are stitched, square up to 8" keeping the circles centered.

STEP 9: Cut directly down the center of each 8" block to make four 4" unfinished squares. (Photo 22)

PHOTO 21

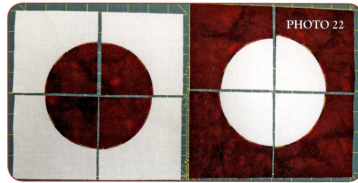

PHOTO 22

YOYO QUILTS

My Aunt Mercedes Tower from Plymouth MA used to make yoyo quilts for all her beds in her Cape Cod home. Yoyo quilts will forever be in my mind as a summer covering for your bed, one that is light and feminine. It is often set in squares with a solid color separating the squares. Auntie Mer's coverlets often had mint green sashings. She grew up in the 1930s so I enjoy making these quilts in 1930s fabrics. Of course, you can make them with any fabrics that you have on hand!

This pretty yoyo quilt belongs to my friend Elise Pennypacker. The bed runner was photographed in front of her Cape Cod home. This beautiful setting reminded me of my Auntie Mer!

This beautiful 30s bedspread was found at an antique store in Putnam CT. I love the on-point setting with two rows of sashing yoyos. To add interest to the edges, the maker added three yoyos that match the center blocks.

Hearts and More is a wonderful tool for cutting circles for making yoyo quilts. You can make several different yoyo quilt sizes and styles. Here are examples of each of the sizes that can be made with the Hearts and More templates. (Photo 23)

The yoyos pictured are the exact finished size when you start with a 5", 4", 3½", 3", 2½", 2", 1⅝", and 1½" circles. The only size I could not make was a yoyo from a 1" circle. The most reasonable size for making a quilt is the 4" or 5" size. The Yoyo Bed Runner in the Project Section of this book (page 63) was made starting with a 5" circle. The yoyos in the Pincushion (page 73) started with 4" circles.

PHOTO 23

What Causes Size Variations in Yoyos?

If you make the stitches too small, the hole in the center will be large and the yoyo will not have a nice appearance. If you make the stitches too large, the yoyo will have too much bulk in the center and will not be round and uniform. Aim for a consistent ¼" stitch. Also, the distance from the edge of the fold to the stitching makes a big difference in the appearance of the finished yoyo. The weight of the fabric contributes to the size of the hole in the center of the yoyo. Very stiff fabric will be harder to gather and will end up with a larger hole. Consistency is key. There is no right or wrong way to make your yoyos as long as they are consistent. Photo 24 shows different size holes in the center of the yoyos.

Note: Make sure your stitches are very secure. You do not want the yoyo to pop open if your stitching lets go.

PHOTO 24

Yoyos: Step by Step

STEP 1: Cut circles four at a time using the instructions on page 19.

STEP 2: Turn under a scant ¼" on the edge of the circle. (Photo 25)

STEP 3: Use a long hand-sewing needle and very strong thread such as hand quilting thread or upholstery thread. Thread your needle with a single thread and make a knot at the end of your thread. With very strong thread there is no need to double the thread. A large knot works best, it will not show on the finished yoyo.

STEP 4: Keep the knot on the top of the folded edge. Start a running stitch keeping stitches evenly spaced approximately ¼" long and ¼" apart. (Photo 25) Continue finger pressing the edge under and continue to stitch all around the edge of the circle. (Photo 26)

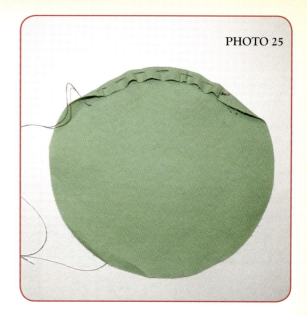

PHOTO 25

STEP 5: When you come back ¼" from the knot, draw up your thread gathering the center of the yoyo. Use your fingers to flatten the yoyo into a circle as you draw the thread tightly in the center. Flatten the yoyo and ensure that the center size is uniform to others that you have made. Once satisfied with the center, tie off the two end threads, one with a knot, and the other longer thread with your needle attached. Use your needle to make a knot in the thread by looping the thread around the needle two times before pulling the knot tight. Once the knot is secure, make a second and a third knot in the same spot, pulling each one tightly. (Photo 27)

PHOTO 26

STEP 6: Trim the threads close to the knot. The thread ends will be inside a fold and will not show.

STEP 7: Once you have made all your yoyos, arrange them in rows and columns. I like to work in either sets of four or sets of nine to make the stitching easier. Some people like to work in complete rows.

Stitch the yoyos together with an overcast stitch by placing the gathered parts together face to face. Choose a spot on the yoyo and catch the two edges together with tiny overcast stitches. Stitches should be closely spaced and pulled tightly. Do not stitch more than ¼" to keep the yoyos circular. If you stitch too much they will look more like squares.

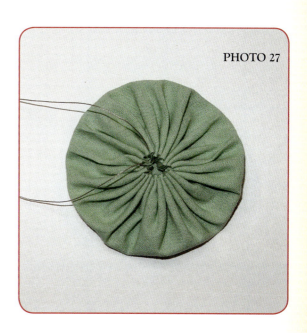

PHOTO 27

Tie off threads carefully. Open up the two yoyos and finger press smooth. Keep adding yoyos together in this manner to make a chain, or make into 2 x 2 or 3 x 3 squares. For square patterns, join the chains or squares together in the same manner making sure to keep the stitching tight, small, and at North, South, East, and West points on each yoyo. (Photo 28)

You can also stitch the yoyos together with a sewing machine. The Yoyo Runner in the Project Section was tacked together by machine. Set your machine to a narrow zigzag stitch. Place yoyos right sides together making sure edges match evenly. Stitch two yoyos together for about ¼" making sure the "zig" to the right is off the edges of the yoyos and the "zag" to the left is about $1/16$" in from the edge. Your stitch to the right will go right off the edges of the yoyo, only the left needle position is on the yoyo. Keep the stitching spaced tightly together and back stitch at each end.

If the yoyos are not all exactly the same size, the zigzag can be adjusted to take a deeper bite out of your yoyos. (Photo 28)

You can also arrange the yoyos in a hexagon pattern with six yoyos touching as in this small table runner. (Photo 29) For this, I used my template to mark six spots on the yoyo 30 degrees apart. Machine tack the yoyos together at each of the six markings using matching thread and a very small zigzag stitch. Putting the yoyos together in this manner is more difficult and it does not leave much room between the yoyos for a background color to show through the holes. This method was used to make the flowers for the Yoyo Pincushion in the Project Section on page 73.

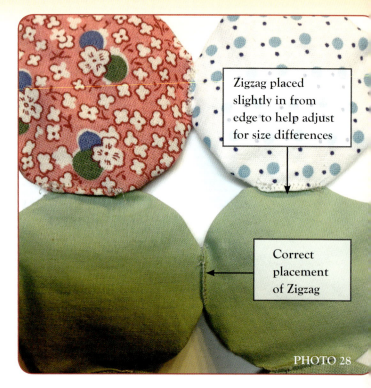

PHOTO 28

PHOTO 29

CHAPTER 6:
Appliqué Stitching and Quilt Finishing Techniques

FINISHING THE EDGES OF FUSED APPLIQUÉ SHAPES

When cutting appliqué shapes from fused fabric, we can iron the shapes wherever we want them to be on our quilts. Most of the time quilters fuse to the background fabric then stitch around each shape with a variety of stitch choices. At other times, quilters choose to apply shapes to a quilted top.

If stitching to background fabric first, the best practice is to use a lightweight tear-away stabilizer behind your background fabric, giving the appliqué edges more stability for stitching. Alternately, you can heavily starch the background fabric to give it body for stitching. Depending on your sewing machine these steps may or may not be necessary. Sometimes the fusible itself between two layers of fabric is enough to stabilize your stitches. As a rule of thumb, if you have to iron after stitching because your piece is no longer flat, you should be using a stabilizer.

Five different stitches are shown in Photos 1 through 6. We used a variegated cotton thread to make it easier for you to see the stitches. When using variegated threads, use a neutral color cotton thread in the

PHOTO 1
Buttonhole Stitch

PHOTO 2
Satin Stitch

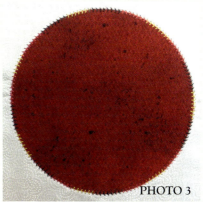
PHOTO 3
Feather Stitch

bobbin of the same weight. Stitch choice is a very important factor when considering how to finish fusible appliqué. You may want to make your own samples of fused shapes like the circles here and experiment with different edge stitches on your machine.

If your goal is to enclose the raw edge to make it less noticeable and to keep the fused edges from fraying, the buttonhole stitch, feather stitch, and satin stitch are all good choices.

A more modern look is to keep the edges raw. With time and washing, the appliqué edges will soften and fray slightly. A straight stitch is ideal for raw edge appliqué.

Occasionally, I will appliqué on quilted fabric to speed up the quilt making process. This method allows me to quilt my background from edge to edge before adding any appliqué shapes. It keeps the cost of professional machine quilting down by eliminating the need for custom quilting. When you plan to quilt first and appliqué after, you must use a cotton batting that can stand up to the heat of fusing the appliqué shapes. Layer your quilt top, cotton batting, and backing and quilt as desired. Add appliqué shapes, then stitch the appliqué with a straight stitch about $1/16$" inside each appliqué shape. Leave both ends of your threads long, tie them off and bury the ends between the layers of batting and backing. The straight stitch around the appliqué adds to the quilting. Because it shows on the back, I do not use any other type of stitch when going through all three layers.

A small zigzag stitch with very fine thread also works well for stitching to a background fabric. I like to use Invisifil for zigzag appliqué, as it holds the edges in better than a straight stitch. In Photo 5 we used a heavy variegated thread so you can see it, but using 100 weight polyester thread the zigzag is barely noticeable.

If you do not like fusible appliqué, you can turn the edges of your shapes under and hand appliqué, or use a nearly invisible stitch on your machine with Invisifil thread, or lightweight clear or smoke color monofilament. Use thin cotton thread in the bobbin, and reduce the tension on the top thread. Step by step instructions for turned-edge appliqué are found on the next page.

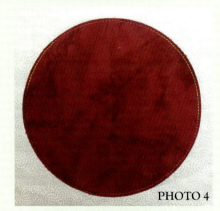
PHOTO 4
Straight Stitch

PHOTO 5
Zigzag Stitch

PHOTO 6
Hand Appliqué

Hand Appliqué or Turned Edge Machine Appliqué: Step by Step

When preparing shapes for hand or turned-edge machine appliqué, use the Hearts and More templates to cut the finished size shapes out of freezer paper. The Hearts and More tools allow you to cut your appliqué freezer paper shapes without tracing and cutting with scissors. This is a real time saver!

STEP 1: Fuse two layers of freezer paper together both with the shiny side down on an appliqué pressing sheet. Fold and cut appliqué shapes from the paper by referring to Chapters 3, 4, and 5. (Photo 7)

STEP 2: Fuse the finished freezer paper shape to the wrong side of fabric. (Photo 8)

STEP 3: Rough cut ¼" larger with scissors. (Photo 9)

STEP 4: Using starch, a glue stick, or your favorite prepared appliqué method, turn under the ¼" seam allowance. (Photo 10)

STEP 5: Pin or baste to background fabric. (Photo 11)

STEP 6: Stitch the appliqué by hand or machine. (Photo 12, zigzag appliqué with monopoly thread; Photo 13, hand appliqué with cotton or silk thread)

STEP 7: Cut a slit in the back of the background fabric and remove the double layer of freezer paper. (Photos 14 and 15)

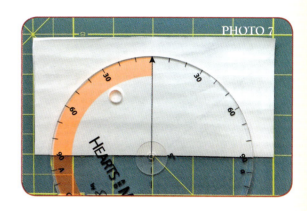
PHOTO 7

PHOTO 8

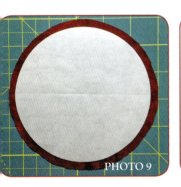
PHOTO 9

PHOTO 10

PHOTO 11

PHOTO 12

PHOTO 13

PHOTO 14

PHOTO 15

SQUARE YOUR QUILTS PRIOR TO BINDING

After quilting, it is very important to carefully square up your quilt prior to binding. If you do not square up your quilt, it is unlikely to hang straight or lie flat. Refer to the printed instructions inside the Quilter's Chalk Line package for more instruction on squaring up quilts.

Standard Binding

Generally, I use a straight-cut binding on straight-edge quilts. For serpentine and scalloped-edge quilts, a bias binding is a must. Refer to my book, "Rotary Cut Appliqué with Leaves Galore Templates" for in depth instructions for finishing quilts with a serpentine or scalloped edge.

And what if you don't want to do a traditional binding? Hearts and More can help you with a variety of edges that do not require binding.

Tab Edge Quilts

Tab edge quilts are most commonly found in wool quilts or penny rugs. Tabs with one rounded end are sewn into a turned quilt so the tabs become the quilt edge rather than having a knife edge. (Photo 16)

PHOTO 16

Appliqué Edge Quilt

This non-traditional binding method is fun to do and a welcome change from traditional bindings.

To make an appliqué edge quilt, choose an appliqué shape that looks nice when it is folded in half. This could be a circle (Photo 17), a leaf (Photo 18), a straight-edge heart, curved-edge heart, (Photo 19) or an oval. Finger press the fusible appliqué shapes in half so both halves are symmetrical.

PHOTO 17

Octagon Table Topper. Designed and Made by Beth Helfter

PHOTO 18

PHOTO 19

Once your quilt is squared up, place the quilt edge on an appliqué pressing sheet. From the front of the quilt, place half of the appliqué shape on the edge of the quilt, with the fold 1/16" over the edge of the quilt. By placing the fold slightly off the edge, you will be able to wrap the edge and keep the shape even on back and front.

Continue to add and fuse appliqué shapes, overlapping each shape by 1/8" to 1/4". Complete one entire edge of the quilt, then peel away the appliqué pressing sheet (if your quilt is large, peel and reposition the sheet until the entire edge is covered). Turn the quilt over and bring the other half of the fusible appliqué shape to the back side of the quilt. Pull snug without distorting the straight edge of the quilt. Fuse in place on the back.

Complete decorative stitching around each shape from the front of the quilt. Beth Helfter used a satin stitch for her Octagon Table Topper. (Photo 17) I like to use a straight stitch to outline each shape.

(Photos 18 and 19) When using the buttonhole and satin stitch it is harder to catch both front and back edges evenly. You can do it, you just need to be very careful when pressing. Straight stitching makes this a bit easier.

QUILTING USING HEARTS AND MORE
Hand Quilting

The Hearts and More tools can be a valuable tool when marking quilting designs. When hand quilting or quilting on a domestic machine, use your Hearts and More tools to mark the quilting design with your favorite marking tool.

Long-Arm Machine Quilting

Long-Arm Machine Quilters will enjoy using the Hearts and More tools for designing quilting designs. However to use the tools as Long-Arm templates, it is necessary to tape two tools of the same size together to make the 1/4" thick templates needed for quilting.

QUILTING DESIGN EXAMPLES

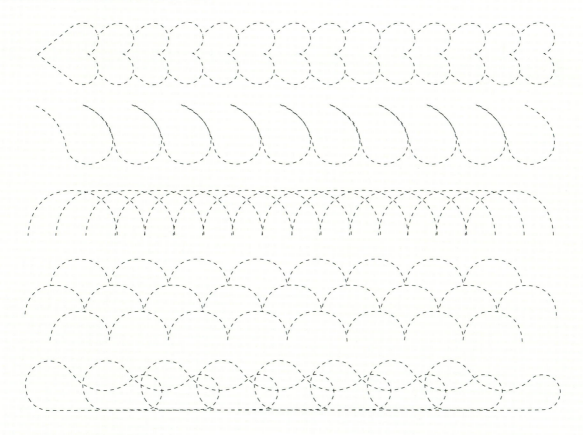

Preface

Please read all instructions before starting the following quilt projects.

Supplies: Most projects require…

- One or more Hearts and More templates
- 28mm rotary cutter with a brand new blade *(I cannot stress this enough, a sharp blade is imperative)*
- A rotating cutting mat if possible
- 6" x 24" acrylic ruler for straight cutting
- Mistyfuse®, or fusible web of your choice
- Appliqué pressing sheet (Fat Goddess Sheet from Mistyfuse)
- Thread to match appliqué
- Thread to match piecing
- A new needle in your machine
- Batting
- Quilter's Chalk Line, marking pencil, or chalk wheel

Fabric: All yardage can be made up of one single fabric or a collection of smaller pieces equal to the total yardage. Many of my quilts are made from a variety of prints to give a scrappy look.

Preparation: Wash and press all fabrics including background fabrics before you begin any project. Review previous chapters on why we need to prepare fabrics properly.

Fusing: Tack each shape in place with the tip of a hot iron. Shapes can then be moved if needed. Cover with a pressing sheet and press with a hot iron for at least 10 seconds to secure permanently. The pressing sheet will keep your fabrics clean in case there is residue on your iron. Turn and press from the back and use steam to ensure a strong bond. Cool completely (at least 15 minutes) before stitching.

Finishing: Square your quilts before binding. Instructions are included in the Quilter's Chalk Line package. Bind with a straight of grain binding if your quilt edge is straight.

Label your quilts so that future generations will know for whom, when, where and why you made your beautiful appliqué quilts. Important information about the quilt maker should be included. At a minimum, include your first name, last name, and maiden name, city, state and the date completed. Include both the quilt top maker and the quilter if they are different. I prefer to stitch my label to the backing fabric, then hand or machine quilt through the label so it cannot be removed.

Lastly, enjoy your quilt! Yes, you have worked long hours to complete this beautiful quilt, but it was not made to be behind glass or in a museum. Love your quilts, snuggle under them with your grandchildren, sleep under them with your hubby, let them comfort you when you are sick. Enjoy your quilts! You can always repair, patch, or recreate your love worn quilts. These are the quilts that will be remembered by future generations, not the quilts that they couldn't touch.

Kaffe Clam Shell Quilt

7" x 97" | *Quilt designed and made by Sue Pelland* | *Quilted by Kathy Sperino*

PROJECT 1:
Kaffe Clam Shell Quilt

MATERIALS LIST

Fabric 1: 4½ yards total of fabrics for appliqué clam shells, flowers, and corners on center of quilt. It is best to use eighteen or more different fat quarters

Fabric 2: 1/8 yard each of at least five to seven green fabrics for leaves and vine

Fabric 3: 7½ yards background fabric

Fusible web: 13 yards, 20" wide Mistyfuse

Backing: 8 yards

Binding: 1 yard

Batting: 98" × 108" or king size

Pattern cutting board

BACKGROUND FABRIC CUTTING CHART

DIAGRAM 1

13½" × 67"	12" × 51"	12" × 101"	4" × 4" squares
13½" × 67"	12" × 51"	12" × 101"	
12" × 91"		12" × 91"	

7½ yards Background = 270"

ASSEMBLY INSTRUCTIONS

Step A: Wash and Press All Fabric

Step B: Cut Background Fabric According to Cutting Chart (Diagram 1)

Cut two of Border 1 at 13½" × 67"

Cut two of Border 1 at 12" × 51"

Cut two of Border 2 at 12" × 101"

Cut two of Border 2 at 12" × 91"

Cut 168 - 4" squares from the remainder of the background fabric

Step C: Prepare Appliqué Fabrics

Fuse all of Fabric 1 for clam shells then cut into 206 - 5" squares. Choose fourteen of the Fabric 1 squares to cut six petal flowers. Reserve the leftover fabric from cutting clam shells to cut circles for flower centers, straight-edge hearts, and straight-edge teardrops for the flower petals. Fuse all of Fabric 2 for leaves and vines.

Step D: Cut Appliqué Shapes

Clam Shells: There are two types of clam shells for this quilt. The inner most clam shell (row 3) is cut into the finished size with no seam allowance with a pointy bottom. (Photo 1) All other clam shells have a ¼" seam allowance on the bottom right and left curved edges with a straight-edge bottom. (Photo 2)

Cut 132 clam shells using the instructions on page 39 for 5" clam shells with a seam allowance. Reserve the 264 curved pieces cut from the two bottom corners. These quarter circles will be used in the center portion of your quilt.

Cut 60 clam shells without a seam allowance using the instructions on page 38. The quarter circles cut from these clam shells are too large for the center of the quilt. You need to cut 24 of these down by ¼" to be added to the pile of corners for Step E. You will need a total of 288 corners.

PHOTO 1

PHOTO 2

Leaves: Cut 330 - 2½" leaves with the Petite Leaves Galore template or use Hearts and More Template C. Cut leaves with the large end of the tool, placing the two 40 degree markings on the fold.

Six-Petal Flowers: Cut five small six-petal flowers. Using Hearts and More Template A small end, place the two 90 degree markings on the fold. Cut seven or eight large six-petal flowers using Hearts and More Template A large end, 70 to 70 degrees on the fold. Use one to make buds. (Photo 3)

Buds: Buds are made from three lobes of six petal flowers and two 2½" or 3" leaves. (Photo 4) Make one to four buds.

Daisy Flower Petals: Using Hearts and More Template A small end from 30 degrees to "Q" to make eight straight-edge petals each of five different fabrics. (Photo 5)

Heart Flowers: Make three different heart-shaped petal flowers. Each flower is made from four straight-edge hearts cut with the Hearts and More Template A small end, placing 90 degrees and "O" on the fold. (Photo 6)

Circles: Use the 1" and 2" circles to make twenty flower centers. I fussy-cut circles from Kaffe Millefiore fabric, that is why my circles are not round. (Photo 6)

PHOTO 3

PHOTO 4

PHOTO 5

PHOTO 6

PHOTO 7

PHOTO 8

Vines: If using the 8" Leaves Galore template use the 8" curve to cut ³⁄₈" wide vine segments from a half yard of fabric. You will need approximately eight vine segments the width of the fabric. If not using Leaves Galore cut approximately sixteen bias strips ³⁄₈" wide diagonally across an 18" square of fabric. In either case, you will splice your vine segments together to make continuous vines around your quilt.

Step E: Center of the Quilt (Diagram 2)

Block 1 (Make 120): Fuse two curved corners cut in Step D (clam shells) to the 4" white squares. (Photo 7)

Block 2 (Make 48): Fuse one curved corner to the remainder of the 4" squares. (Photo 8)

Stitch the curved edges on all squares using a decorative machine stitch.

Step F: Lay the Blocks out into a Center Panel

Lay out the center section of the quilt using a grid of 12 × 14 blocks. Use Block 2 as indicated to make a diagonal design (Diagram 2). Sew the squares together by row and press each row to make opposing seams for ease of construction. Sew the rows together making the quilt center as shown. (Diagram 2)

Step G: Baste Unfused Borders to Quilt Center

Using the two 12" × 51" borders, center the border on the quilt center leaving ½" overhang on each end of the quilt. Baste with a long machine stitch. Center the 13½" × 67" border on the quilt center leaving ½" overhang. Baste to the quilt center leaving the seams open from the corner of the quilt center to the edge of the quilt. (Photo 9 and Diagram 3)

The temporary basting will be removed after arranging and fusing all four borders. The decorative stitching around the appliqué shapes sometimes makes your borders shrink in a bit, so we have a little extra border length to make them fit perfectly in the end.

Step H: Arrange Appliqué Shapes (Photo 10)

Loosely follow the appliqué placement on the quilt. (page 53) Place your curved vine segments or bias strips and tack vines in place by lightly tapping with the tip of a hot iron every inch or two. Do not fuse just yet, you may need to make adjustments or trim vines that flow under flowers.

When you come to the corner of the quilt, tack the vines into the excess length on the border. If needed, we will trim this excess border later after our decorative stitching is done. Be very careful to match the vines at the corners to make them flow around the quilt. Once you place your main vine, arrange off-shoots from the vine in any open areas.

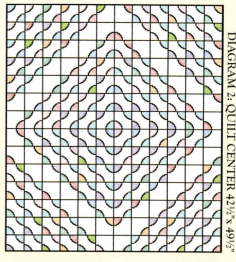

DIAGRAM 2: QUILT CENTER 42½" × 49½"

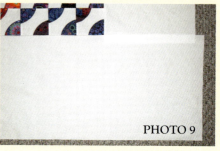

PHOTO 9

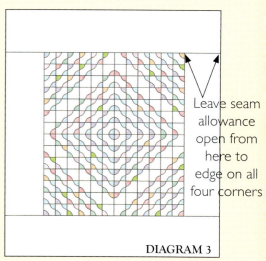

Leave seam allowance open from here to edge on all four corners

DIAGRAM 3

PHOTO 10

Branches come off the main vine at approximately a 45 degree angle and in a clockwise pattern to make the vines look like they are growing around the quilt center. Vines do not need to be symmetrical or perfectly spaced around the center panel. Use your own creativity and design sense to make the vine your own and have fun with this!

Once the vines are placed and meet well in the corners, start to place flowers randomly around the border. Make sure you have a good mix of six-petal flowers, eight-petal daisies, heart-shaped petal flowers, and buds around the quilt. Try to avoid symmetry, but instead look for balance of colors and shapes as you place the flowers. Stay about ½" away from the corner seams that are not sewn. Reserve flowers and leaves to place over the seams once all four borders are sewn with decorative stitching. Tack the flowers and petals in place. Trim any vines that show through the flower fabrics. Tuck leaves around and behind the flowers and on both sides of the vine always moving in a clockwise pattern. Trim any leaves that show through light-colored flowers.

On the back of the borders, mark the top border with a small "t", the bottom border with a small "b" etc, so it will be easy to reassemble the quilt. Remove basting stitches. Give your appliqués a hot press. Turn the border over and press from the wrong side. Steam if needed to fuse the appliqués in place.

Sew decorative stitching around all design elements using matching threads. We used a buttonhole stitch on the cover quilt. Change threads as needed. Bring all thread ends to the back of the quilt, tie off, and weave through the back of the stitches.

Step I: Reassemble the Quilt Top

Reassemble the quilt top starting with the left and right borders centering the borders as before. This time sew with a regular length stitch. Center and sew top and bottom borders all the way from edge to edge without leaving the corners open this time.

Add leaves and flowers as needed to cover any vines that do not match. Sew decorative stitching around these design elements. (Photo 10)

This portion of the quilt needs to measure 65½" x 75½". Adjust if needed.

Step J: Clam Shell Border

Using one of the 12" x 101" Border 2, fold the border in half to find the center of the 101" length. Place the border on a pattern cutting board starting with the top of the border on a solid grid line, keeping the center of the border on a 1" marking. Mark the center of the border with a T-pin. We will be using grid lines 2½" apart on the pattern cutting board. Starting in the center of the border, line up eighteen clam shells keeping the top of the clam shell on the line 2" from the top of the border, and the bottom of the clam shell 7" from the top of the border. There are an even number of clam shells, so you will have two clam shells coming together on the center marking on the border. (Photo 11)

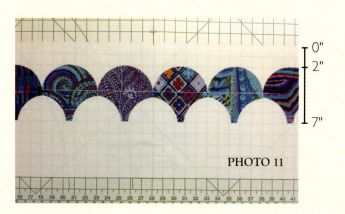

PHOTO 11

Use a chalk line to mark this first row of eighteen clam shells 2¼" below the top of the first row. Line up the second row of seventeen clam shells on this line overlapping the curved top edge by ¼" over the bottom edges of the first row. Make sure the bottom of the clam shells line up ¼" below the straight line on the pin board. (Photo 12)

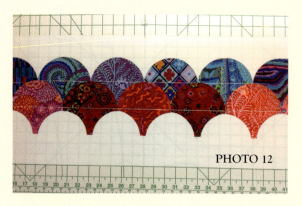

PHOTO 12

Measure down again 2½" from the top of the second row. Add a third row of sixteen clam shells in the same way, making sure you use the Row 3 clam shells that you cut in Step D. These clam shells come to a point on the bottom and complete the clam shell look right on the ¼" seam line. It is very important to make sure the two sides of each clam shell come together into a smooth half circle with no fabric showing from the clam shells above. The point of this last row should come exactly ¼" from the bottom edge of the border. (Photo 13)

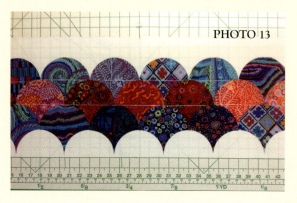

PHOTO 13

Once all three rows of clam shells are fused, complete decorative stitching around the top of each clam shell in each row with a continuous line of decorative stitching. Make a second side border.

Repeat with the 12" x 91" Border 2 for the top and bottom of the quilt using sixteen in Row 1, fifteen in Row 2 and fourteen in Row 3.

Sew all four borders on the quilt, start and end stitching ¼" from raw edges of quilt, backstitching at each end.

Step K: Miter the Clam Shell Border
Lay the quilt face up on your ironing board. Fold both quilt borders back at a 45 degree angle from the last stitch. Make a hard crease with the iron. Fold the quilt on the diagonal, right sides together. Line up raw edges of the border and the crease lines. Pin. Sew from the edge of the borders into the corner of the quilt making sure to stop exactly at the last stitch on both borders. Unfold the quilt top and check to make sure there are no puckers at the quilt corner. Trim mitered seam to ¼". Press the seam open. Repeat for all corners. (Diagram 4)

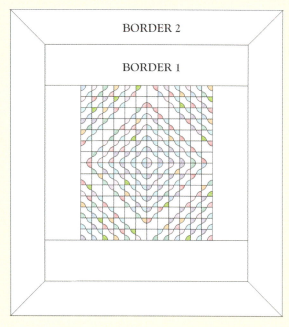

DIAGRAM 4

The clam shells will not come all the way to the mitered seam and will have raw edges. We will fill the gap with leaves in the next step.

Step L: Appliqué Over Mitered Seams

Cut 3" leaves to fill the corner. Use Hearts and More Template C, large end, 40 to 50 degrees on fold.

You may need to adjust the size of the leaves to fit exactly in your corners. (Photo 14) Make the leaves slightly larger or smaller as you fit them into the corner one at a time. Once you have fused three leaves over the mitered seam, complete the decorative stitching around each leaf.

Step M: Quilt Finishing

Make a backing. Layer quilt top, batting, and backing. Baste and quilt as desired. Square up your quilt, bind, label, and enjoy!

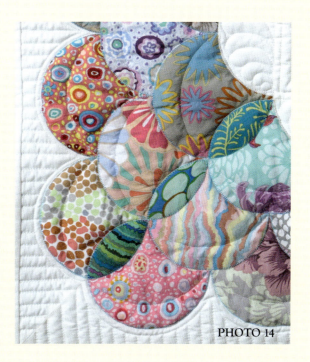

PHOTO 14

Blue Moons
52" x 64" | Quilt made by Joanne Bertrand and Sue Pelland | Quilted by Shirley Tetreault

PROJECT 2: Blue Moons

MATERIALS LIST

Fabric 1: 1½ yards for Moons, Border 1, and piping. We used SewBatik's Nuance Gradation Batik in Yellow. This fabric is shaded from dark to light from selvedge to selvedge.

Fabric 2: 1¾ yards for Border 2, binding, and alternating blocks (without the moons)

Fabric 3: 1½ yards for Border 3. Use the leftover fabric as one of the celestial prints for squares.

Optional: 4 fat quarters of celestial prints for more variety

Fusible web: 1 yard, 20" wide Mistyfuse

Backing: 3⅓ yards of 42" wide fabric

Batting: 60" x 72"

CUTTING INSTRUCTIONS

Cut 18 – 6" squares of Fabric 1

Cut 17 – 6¾" squares of Fabric 2

Cut 18 – 6¾" squares of Fabric 3 (or a variety of fat quarters of celestial print fabrics)

Cut 18 – 6" squares of Mistyfuse

Border 1, Fabric 1: cut 4 @ 1½" x length of fabric (along selvedge edge) Actual border size measured in Step J.

Border 2, Fabric 2: cut 4 @ 3" x length of fabric (along selvedge edge) Actual border size measured in Step K.

Border 3, Fabric 3: cut 4 @ 7½" x length of fabric (along selvedge edge) Actual border size measured in Step K.

ASSEMBLY INSTRUCTIONS

Step A: Wash and Press All Fabric

Step B: Center Mistyfuse and press to the back of the eighteen squares of Fabric 3 (or a mix of celestial print fabrics) using an appliqué pressing sheet. (Photo 1)

PHOTO 1

PHOTO 2

Step C: Finger press squares in quarters or mark with iron-erase chalk in both directions. Cut a 5" circle out of the fused squares using Template D, large end. (Photo 2)

Step D: Keeping these circles folded, cut a 4" circle from the center of the 5" circle using Template C, large end. (Photo 3)

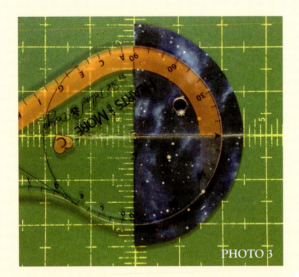
PHOTO 3

Step E: With the 6¾" square face down, center the 6" square of Fabric 1 over the fusible web. (Photo 4) Cover with an appliqué pressing sheet and fuse.

Step F: Use one of the 4" circles from the same fabric and fuse the 4" circle inside the 5" circle cut out, just touching the outside circle at one point. (Photo 5) Randomly place the circles so they are all touching at different points. Make eighteen moon blocks.

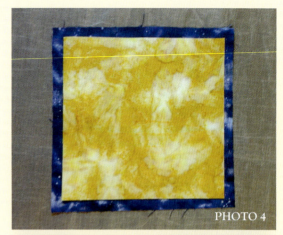
PHOTO 4

PHOTO 5

Step G: Keep the 5" rings for a future project or use them on the back of this quilt project (see how to make a chain in Chapter 4).

Step H: Stitch around the fused raw edges of all the circles using a decorative machine stitch.

Step I: Sew the quilt top alternating Fabric 2 squares with the fused and stitched moon squares.

Step J: Measure center panel. Cut Border 1 the same length as the center panel. Add these two side borders first. Measure width of center panel and Border 1. Cut two Border 1 the same size as the quilt width. Add to top and bottom of quilt center.

Step K: Repeat with Borders 2 and 3.

Step L: Make a backing. Layer quilt top, batting, and backing. Baste and quilt as desired. Square up your quilt, bind, label, and enjoy!

Note: We used the Piping Hot Binding method by Susan Cleveland to add a very small piping next to the quilt binding.

Yoyo Bed Runner

42" x 72" | *Quilt made by Sue Pelland and Joanne Bertrand*

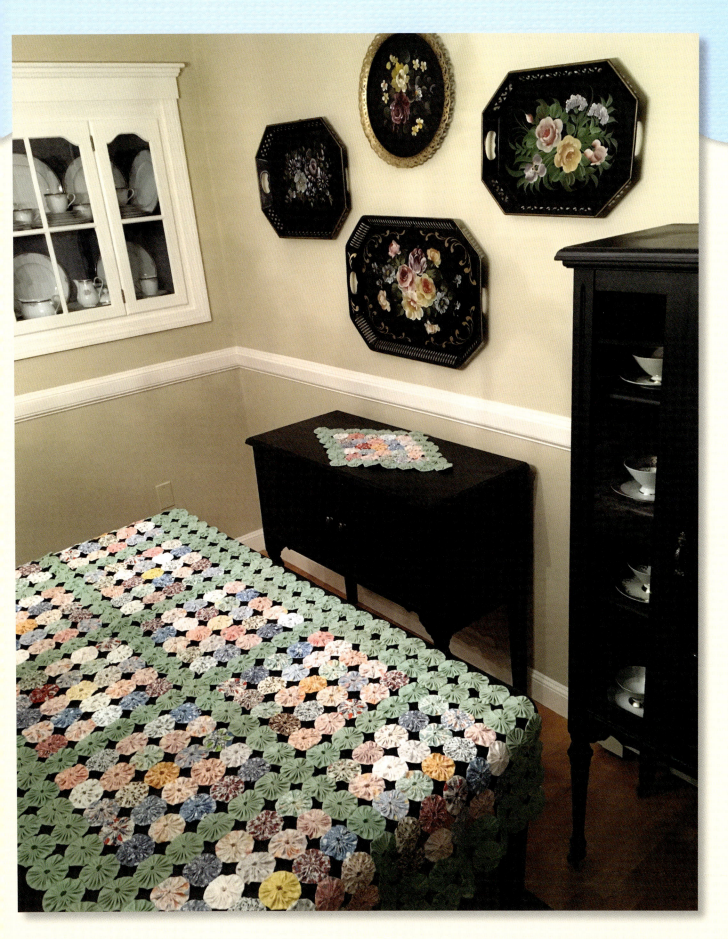

PROJECT 3:
Yoyo Bed Runner

Read about Yoyo Quilts in Chapter 5, Special Quilts. The bed runner is made from 10 squares of 25 yoyos in a 5 x 5 pattern.

The squares are separated by one row of green sashing yoyos. A border of two full rows of yoyos surrounds the bed runner.

MATERIALS LIST

Fabric 1: 5¼ yards for block colors (assorted 30s reproduction prints in cover quilt)

Fabric 2: 4¼ yards for sashing color (green in cover quilt)

Heavy duty thread such as upholstery thread. Hand quilting thread is not strong enough.

Hand sewing needle, fairly long

ASSEMBLY INSTRUCTIONS

Step A: Wash and Press All Fabric

Step B: Cut 250 - 5¼" squares of Fabric 1 and cut 195 - 5¼" squares of Fabric 2.

Step C: Cut 5" circles from the center of all 5¼" squares as follows: Layer four 5¼" squares on a rotating cutting mat. Center the 5" circle (Template D) on the squares. (Photo 1)

PHOTO 1

Cut more than half way around the circle then rotate the template and the mat to line up the cut line with the circle outline on the tool. Continue the cut to make full 5" circles. (Photo 2)

PHOTO 2

Step D: Follow instructions on page 45 for stitching around the circles to make the yoyos. Stitch all yoyos. (Photo 3)

PHOTO 3

Step E: Stitch yoyos into rows of five, then stitch five rows together into blocks of twenty-five yoyos. (Photo 4)

Step F: Stitch twenty-five rows of five sashing color yoyos.

Step G: Stitch eight rows of fifteen sashing color yoyos.

Step H: Sew one row of five sashing color yoyos between blocks. (Photo 5) Sew two rows of five sashing color yoyos to each end. (Photo 6)

Step I: Stitch one row of fifteen sashing yoyos between rows. (Photo 7)

Step J: Stitch two rows of fifteen sashing yoyos on either end of runner. (Photo 7)

Note: Some quilters like to back yoyo quilts by tacking it to a solid color backing. I prefer to lay the runner over a colored bed covering. This way, the color of the bed covering can be changed and the color will show through the openings in the yoyo quilt. If you place the yoyos over a dark bedcover, you can see the dark color between yoyos. (page 63) Photo 7 shows a light pink bedcover under the yoyo quilt for a soft, feminine look.

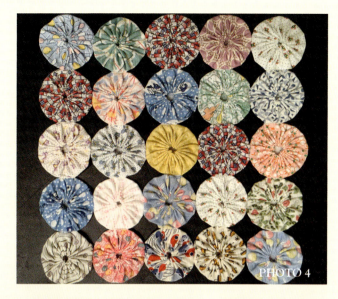
PHOTO 4

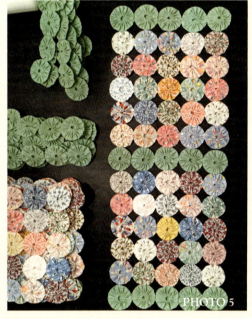
PHOTO 5

PHOTO 6

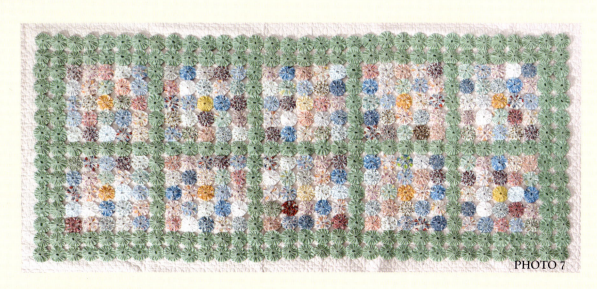
PHOTO 7

Mediterranean Blues

64" x 80" | Quilt designed and made by Sue Pelland | Quilted by Shirley Tetreault

PROJECT 4: Mediterranean Blues

MATERIALS LIST

Fabric 1: 4 yards light colors. This could be eight half yards or sixteen regular quarters or twenty fat quarters

Fabric 2: 2½ yards dark colors. This could be five half yards or ten regular quarters or twelve fat quarters

Fusible web: 6 yards, 20" wide Mistyfuse

Backing: 5 yards

Binding: ¾ yard

Batting: 72" × 88"

ASSEMBLY INSTRUCTIONS

Step A: Wash and Press All Fabric

Step B: Prepare the Fabrics

Fabric 1: Cut 80 - 8" light colored squares. Of the light colored background squares, cut 48 diagonally to make 96 triangles.

Fabric 2: Fuse the back of the dark fabrics. From fused fabric cut 48 - 8" squares.

Step C: Cut Fused Fabrics

One at a time, fold the Fabric 2 squares fusible side in on the diagonal and place on a rotating cutting mat.

Using Template D, large end, place the straight line ending with an arrow on the raw edges, the 90 degree marking on the fold, and the circle line on the point. (Photo 1)

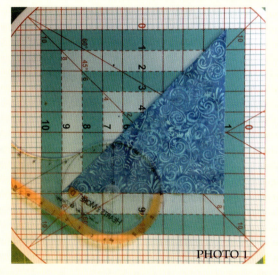

PHOTO 1

Cut the curve from 90 degree to Zero (the arrow) with a sharp 28mm rotary cutter blade. Repeat for the opposite point so you are cutting off the two corners diagonally across from each other. (Photo 2)

PHOTO 2

Place the center piece in one pile and the two heart-shaped pieces in another pile.

Step D: Assemble Blocks

Block 1 (Make 48): To assemble blocks with the dark center, place a center piece fusible side up on your ironing board. Place a light triangle right side down with the diagonal lined up from point to point on the center piece. Keep cut edges even. (Photo 3) Place a second triangle of a different light fabric in the same manner to make an 8" square. Press the two triangles to the back of the fused fabric center piece. (Photo 4)

Turn and press from the front. (Photo 5)

Block 2 (Make 24): To assemble blocks with a light center, place an 8" light square right side up on your ironing board. Place two different heart-shaped pieces fusible side down on two opposite corners lining up raw edges. Fuse. (Photo 6)

Stitch the fused edges of both block types with a buttonhole stitch or other decorative machine stitch.

Step E: Quilt Assembly

Lay out quilt center using the dark-center blocks, 6 x 8. Lay out one row of light-center blocks all around the 6 x 8 center to make a border. Final layout is 8 x 10. (See Cover Photo)

Sew blocks together into horizontal rows of eight blocks each. Press seams open to reduce bulk. Join ten horizontal rows to complete the quilt top. Press seams open.

Step F: Quilt Finishing

Make a backing. Layer quilt top, batting, and backing. Baste and quilt as desired. Square up your quilt, bind, label, and enjoy!

PHOTO 3

PHOTO 4

PHOTO 5

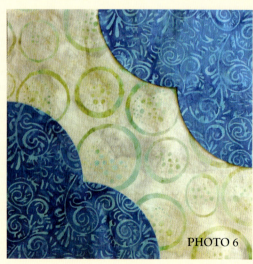
PHOTO 6

Sienna Rooftops

4" x 63" | *Quilt made by Sue Pelland and Elaine Nadeau | Quilted by Linda Gosselin*

PROJECT 5:
Sienna Rooftops

MATERIALS LIST

Fabric 1: A total of 3¼ yards light colors. This could be eight half yards or fifteen fat quarters. Do not use quarter yard cuts, (9" x 40") as there is too much waste.

Fabric 2: A total of 1¾ yards dark colors. This could be four half yards or eight fat quarters. Do not use quarter yard cuts, (9" x 40") as there is too much waste.

Fusible web: 4 yards, 20" wide Mistyfuse

Backing: 3 yards

Binding: ½ yard

Batting: 62" x 71"

ASSEMBLY INSTRUCTIONS

Step A: Wash and Press All Fabric

Step B: Prepare the Fabric
Fabric 1: Cut 168 - 5" light colored squares. Of the 168 - 5" light colored background squares of Fabric 1, cut 80 diagonally to make 160 triangles.

Fabric 2: Fuse the back of Fabric 2. Cut 88 - 5" squares.

Step C: Cut Corners of Fused Squares
One at a time, fold the Fabric 2 squares (fusible side in) on the diagonal and place on a rotating cutting mat. Using Template D small end, place the straight line ending with an arrow on the raw edges of the fabric square, the 90 degree marking on the fold, and the circle line on the point of the folded piece. (Photo 1)

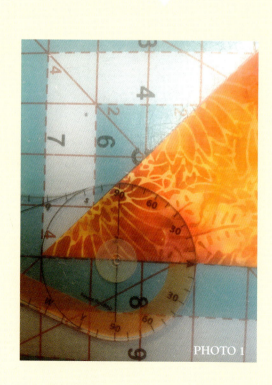
PHOTO 1

Cut the curve from 90 degree to Zero (the arrow) with a sharp 28mm rotary cutter blade. Repeat for the opposite point so you are cutting off the two corners that are diagonally across from each other. Place the dark center piece in one pile and the two heart-shaped pieces in another pile. (Photo 2)

Step D: Assemble Blocks

Block 1 (Make 80): To assemble blocks with the dark center, place a dark center piece fusible side up on your ironing board. Place a light triangle right side down with the diagonal lined up from point to point on the center piece. Keep cut edges even. (Photo 3)

Place a second triangle of a different fabric in the same manner to make a 5" square. Press the two triangles to the back of the fused fabric center piece. (Photo 4) Turn over and press from the front. You will have extra dark center pieces.

Block 2 (Make 88): To assemble blocks with a light center, place a 5" light square right side up on your ironing board. Place two different heart-shaped fused pieces on two opposite corners and fuse. (Photo 5)

PHOTO 2

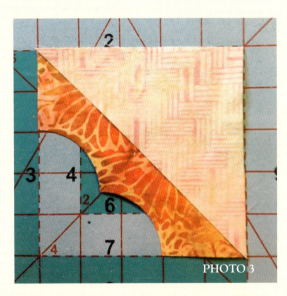

PHOTO 3

PHOTO 4

PHOTO 5

Stitch the fused edges of both block types with a buttonhole stitch or other decorative machine stitch.

Lay out quilt center using dark center blocks, 8 × 10 grid. Arrange two rows of light center blocks to form a border all around the quilt center. (Photo 6)

Sew blocks together into fourteen horizontal rows with twelve blocks in each row. Press seams open between blocks. Join horizontal rows to complete the quilt top. Press seams open.

Step E: Quilt Finishing

Make a backing. Layer quilt top, batting, and backing. Baste and quilt as desired. Square up your quilt, bind, label, and enjoy!

PHOTO 6

Candy Dish Pincushion
Made by Sue Pelland

PROJECT 6: Candy Dish Pincushion

An antique candy dish can be made into a useful and beautiful pincushion. Look for a pretty candy dish or ice cream dish in your local secondhand or antique shops. Many different types are available! The color of this blue/green candy dish and the size was perfect for a pincushion. The pillow is removable so you can use it with or without the dish. Under the pillow, I store odd pins such as T-pins or sewing machine needles. The pretty top section of the pincushion is reserved for my favorite flower head pins.

Read the Yoyo Section of Chapter 5 before you begin.

MATERIALS LIST

Antique candy dish, 4½" to 6" diameter. If larger or smaller, adjust sizes accordingly.

One 15" square background fabric

Six 5" squares fabric for yoyo flower

One 5" square fabric for flower center

One 8" square fabric for leaves

Heavy weight chipboard or cardboard (not corrugated), cut into a 4" circle (Template C)

Mistyfuse cut into a 4" circle (Template C)

Heavy weight upholstery thread

1½ cups dry white rice, sand box sand, or walnut shell filling

Fiberfil

Hand sewing needle

ASSEMBLY INSTRUCTIONS

Step A: Cut six 5" circles of flower fabric and one from flower center fabric.

Step B: Make the seven yoyos for the flower as in Chapter 5, page 45.

Step C: Cut a 15" circle using the pattern on page 97 out of the background fabric. I used solid white fabric for the pincushion "pillow".

Step D: Sew around the 15" circle by hand just as you would a smaller yoyo, turning under ¼" on the edge of the circle. Make sure you use a very heavy thread such as hand quilting thread or upholstery thread.

Step E: Center the Mistyfuse circle then the chipboard circle on the wrong side of the 15" circle. Fuse in place. Flip circle over and press from the fabric side. Let cool completely. (Photo 1)

PHOTO 1

Step F: Gather the center hole slightly then add 1½ cups of dry white rice to add weight to the pillow.

Step G: Start adding fiberfil small bits at a time to prevent lumps (Hint: pull the fiberfil apart between two hands to fluff the fibers as if you were pulling taffy. This will eliminate lumps.)

Step H: Place the "pillow" inside your candy dish to keep filling to make a snug fit. Compress the fiberfil as you stuff to make a dense pillow. Keep gathering the circle until the hole is centered and the pillow is mounded with fiberfil. It should look like a large scoop of ice cream! Once you have stuffed it completely, gather the center tightly by pulling on both ends of your heavy thread. Tie several knots in place to close up the center hole. (Photo 2)

PHOTO 2

Step I: Arrange the flower yoyos around the center yoyo. One at a time, fold each flower yoyo over the center yoyo. Overcast a small area approximately ¼" to create the flower center. Once all the flower yoyos are sewn to the center, fold each petal right sides together with the adjacent petal, and overcast the edge where they meet. You can also zigzag together by machine. (Photo 3)

PHOTO 3

Step J: Cut six 4" leaves with the Leaves Galore Grande template (optional) or use the pattern on page 98. Place two leaves right sides together and straight stitch around the edges. Make a small slit in the back of one layer of the leaf toward one end and turn the leaf right sides out. Gently push out the point. (Photo 4) Gather or pleat the wide end of the leaf. (Photo 5)

PHOTO 4   PHOTO 5

Step K: Once the flower is completely sewn, place the flower center on top of the pincushion pillow, covering the gathered top of the pillow. Tuck leaves up under flower. Sew the leaves and flower down to the pincushion using a blind stitch or appliqué stitch. (page 73) Enjoy!

Drunkard's Path
38" x 38" | Drunkard's Path Flying Birds variation made by Sue Pelland | Quilted by Shirley Tetreault

PROJECT 7: Drunkard's Path

FLYING BIRDS OR WINDING WAYS

One Flying Birds block

Four Flying Birds blocks

DIAMONDS OR WEDDING RING

One Diamond block

Four Diamond blocks

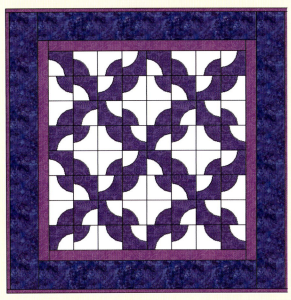

DIAGRAM 1

DIAGRAM 2

DRUNKARD'S PATH VARIATIONS

Two Drunkard's Path variations are shown on this page. Each quilt has the same fabric requirements and cutting steps. The only difference is in the arrangement of four squares to make a block. Follow the diagrams above to make both block variations.

MATERIALS LIST

Fabric 1: ¾ yard light fabric

Fabric 2: 1 yard dark fabric

Fabric 3: ½ yard contrasting fabric for Border 1 and Binding

Fusible web: ⅓ yard, 20" wide Mistyfuse

Backing: 1¼ yards 45" wide fabric, cut into a 45" square

Batting: 45" x 45"

ASSEMBLY INSTRUCTIONS

Step A: Wash and Press All Fabric

Step B: Precut the fabric

Fabric 1: Light Fabric

　Cut eight 6" squares

　Cut eight 8¼" squares

Fabric 2: Dark Fabric

　Cut eight 8¼" squares

　Cut four 4" × WOF strips for Border 2

Fabric 3: Contrasting Fabric

　Cut four 1½" × WOF strips for Border 1

　Cut five 2¼" × WOF strips for binding

Fusible Web: Cut eight 6" squares Mistyfuse

Step C: Follow step by step instructions for Drunkard's Path in Chapter 5, page 42 using eight each of the dark and light squares, eight 6" light squares and eight 6" Mistyfuse squares. You will make a total of 32 dark background squares and 32 light background squares. (Photo 1)

Step D: Using two light background squares and two dark background squares assemble blocks with either the Flying Birds variation or the Diamonds variation. Make sixteen identical blocks of either Unit 1 or Unit 2. (Diagrams 3 and 4)

PHOTO 1

Diagram 3
Unit 1

Diagram 4
Unit 2

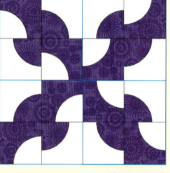

Diagram 5
Unit 3

Diagram 6
Unit 4

Step E: Following either Diagram 5 or Diagram 6, sew four blocks together, rotating blocks as needed. Make four of Unit 3 as in Diagram 1. Make four of Unit 4 as in Diagram 2.

Step F: Sew four of Unit 3 or four of Unit 4 together to make the pieced quilt top shown in Diagrams 1 and 2.

Step G: Measure the width of the pieced quilt top and cut two of Border 1 to that exact measurement. Sew Border 1 onto the two sides of the pieced quilt top.

Step H: Measure the piece quilt top including the two side borders. Cut two of Border 1 to that exact measurement. Sew to the top and bottom of the pieced top.

Step I: Repeat Steps E and F for Border 2.

Step J: Make a backing. Layer quilt top, batting, and backing. Baste and quilt as desired. Square up your quilt, bind, label, and enjoy!

Enough Love to Go Around

0" x 60" | Designed by Sue Pelland | Made by Sue Pelland and Akiko Kunst | Quilted by Kathy Sperino

PROJECT 8: Enough Love to Go Around

VERSION 1

The dark gray quilt is Version 1, which uses the Leaves Galore Norme and Petite templates in addition to Hearts and More Templates A and B.

The black print version with rainbow colors is Version 2, which uses only the small set of Hearts and More templates. (Templates A and B)

VERSION 2

The difference between Version 1 and Version 2 is the way you cut the teardrop shaped leaves for the Crossed Branches block and the standard leaves on the Heart Wreath and Swag Border blocks. In Version 1, the leaves are made with the Leaves Galore Norme template, then one end of the leaves are rounded with the small Hearts and More Template A (Photo 1) resulting in a more rounded shape for the teardrops. (Photo 2)

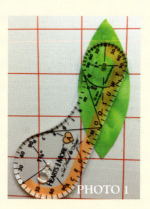

PHOTO 1

PHOTO 2

Version 1 utilizes the Petite Leaves Galore template to make the leaves for the Heart Wreath blocks since it is faster to make standard leaves with Leaves Galore. The same size leaves can be made with Hearts and More.

Version 1 uses the Leaves Galore template to cut curved stems for the Heart Wreath blocks and for the Swag Border blocks.

Version 2 uses the teardrop shape and leaf shape made with the Hearts and More template only. Use the leaf cutting instructions for Version 2 if you do not yet own the Leaves Galore templates.

MATERIALS LIST

Version 1: All hearts and flowers are the same three dark, medium, and light fabrics

Fabric 1: ½ yard Dark (pink in cover quilt)

Fabric 2: ¼ yard Medium (pink in cover quilt)

Fabric 3: ½ yard Light (pink in cover quilt)

Fabric 4: 1 yard total (a collection of green fabrics for appliqué leaves and stems)

Version 2: A wide variety of colors for hearts and flowers. We used eight color families, with light, medium, and dark in each color family. (Photo 3) We used one green fabric throughout the quilt, SewBatik's Nuance Gradation in Mint.

Fabric 1: Cut eight 11" × 11" squares (Dark shade of eight different colors)

Fabric 2: Cut eight 4" × 8" rectangles (Medium shade of eight different colors)

Fabric 3: Cut eight 7" × 8" rectangles (Light shade of eight different colors)

Fabric 4: 1 yard total (one fabric or a collection of green fabrics for appliqué leaves and stems)

For Both Versions:

Background fabric: $4^{5}/_{8}$ yards

Backing: 4 yards

Binding: ½ yard

Batting: 70" square

Fusible web: 5 yards, 20" wide Mistyfuse

ASSEMBLY INSTRUCTIONS

Step A - Version 1 and 2: Wash and Press All Fabric

Step B - Version 1 and 2: Prepare Fabric

Fuse the back of all appliqué fabrics with Mistyfuse (greens and pinks in Version 1; rainbow colors and greens in Version 2).

Step C - Version 1 and 2: Cut Background Fabric

Inside border: Cut four 48½" × 2¾" strips. Background squares for Crossed Branches blocks and Heart Wreath blocks: Cut nine 15" squares.

Background rectangles for Swag Border blocks: Cut sixteen 12½" × 6½" rectangles.

Corner stones: Cut four 6½" squares.

PHOTO 3

Step D - Versions 1 and 2: Cut Hearts and Flowers from Fused Fabrics

Cut two squares from each color family for six petal flowers according to Table 1. Follow the instructions on page 33 to cut the flowers using the template and markings in Table 1:

TABLE 1: CUTTING FLOWERS (PHOTO 4)

Fabric color	Cut Fabric	Version One	Version Two	Template	End(in)	Place on fold
Dark	4½" square	Cut 16	2 each of 8 different colors	A	1⅝	70°
Medium	3½" square	Cut 16		A	1	90°
Light	2½" square	Cut 16		A	1	60°

PHOTO 4

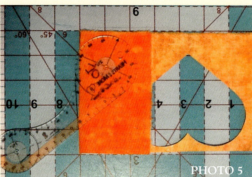
PHOTO 5

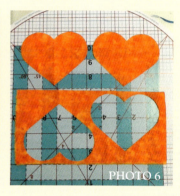
PHOTO 6

TABLE 2: CUTTING HEARTS (PHOTOS 5 AND 6)

Fabric color	Cut Fabric	Version One	Version Two	Template	End(in)	Place on fold
Dark	10" × 5"	Cut 16	2 each of 8 different colors	B	2½	80° and N
Light	7" × 3½"	Cut 16		A	1⅝	90° and Q

Step E - Version 1: Crossed Branches Blocks

Stems: From one rectangle of fused green fabric 14"× 5", cut ten stems ⅜" wide by 14" long.

Teardrops: Cut 120 – 3" leaves with Leaves Galore Norme template. Keeping leaves in stacks of four, round the ends of the leaves with Hearts and More Template A, small end. (Photo 7)

PHOTO 7

Step E - Version 2: Crossed Branches Blocks

Stems: From one rectangle of green fabric 14"x 5", cut ten stems using one green fabric 3/8" wide by 14" long.

Teardrops: Cut 120 teardrops with Hearts and More Template A, small end, Zero degrees to the small letter "I". (Photo 8)

Step F - Version 1: Cut Curved Stems and Leaves for Heart Wreath Blocks and Swag Border Blocks

Curved Stems: From green fabric cut a 6" x 22" fused rectangle, cut 48 stems for blocks and borders. Cut the stems using the Norme Leaves Galore template, approximately 3/8" wide. Line up the "i" with bottom of fabric and the top of the "a" at the peak of the template with the cut edge of the curve. Judge the width by eye or use the lines on your cutting board. (Photos 9 and 10)

PHOTO 8

Leaves: Cut 240 - 2½" leaves using the Leaves Galore Petite template (80 leaves for Wreath blocks and 160 leaves for Swag border). Use the instructions for the Leaves Galore template or use the online video to learn to cut standard leaves.

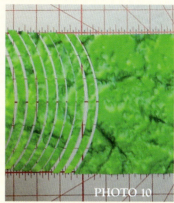

PHOTO 9   PHOTO 10

Step F - Version 2: Cut Stems and Leaves for Heart Wreath Blocks and Swag Border Blocks

Stems: From a 5" x 30" rectangle, cut 48 strips 3/8" wide on the bias of your fabric rectangle. To do this cut a triangle from the 6" end of your fabric to make a 45 degree angle. Cut strips along the 45 degree angle. (Photo 11)

Leaves: Cut 240 - 2½" leaves using the Hearts and More Template C, large end, 40 to 40 degrees . (Photo 12) Use 80 leaves for Wreath blocks and 160 leaves for the Swag Border blocks.

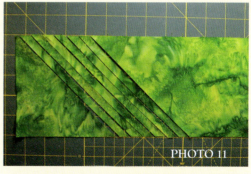

PHOTO 11

Step G - Versions 1 and 2: Arrange Appliqué Elements on Background Fabric

Heart Wreath block (Make 4): Tack together one dark heart with one light heart in the center on appliqué pressing sheet. (Photo 13) Fold background square in quarters and lightly finger press. Use a 10½" circle on pattern page 97 and arrange curved stems as in Diagram 1.

PHOTO 12

If using bias strips, gently tack the stems over the 10½" circle as in Diagram 1, curving bias stems around the circle with the outside edge on the 10½" line. Place the hearts between curved stems then trim the ends of the stems so they don't show through the light-colored hearts. (Photo 13) Remove hearts and fuse stems. Place and fuse leaves. Stitch stems and leaves. Add hearts. Stitch. Square up to 14½". (Photo 14)

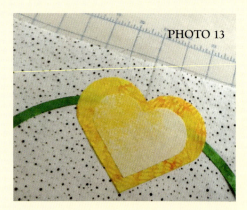

PHOTO 13

Crossed Branches block (Make 5): Fold background square in fourths on the diagonal. Place stems on diagonal fold lines. Place teardrop shapes along the stems at equal intervals and at the end of each stem according to Diagram 2. Fuse and stitch appliqué. Square up to 14½".

Swag Border block (Make 16): Fold rectangle in quarters and finger press. Mark a ¼" line on bottom and short sides of rectangle. (Diagram 3) Use iron-erasable chalk or a Frixion pen. Place outside edge of arcs on the ¼" line making sure the arc crosses both ¼" seam lines. (Diagram 3) Add leaves, fuse, and stitch. Make three part flowers on an appliqué pressing sheet. Add flowers and stitch. Blocks will measure 12½"x 6½".

PHOTO 14

Step H - Quilt Assembly (Diagram 4)

Piece blocks together in three rows of three. Press seams so they are opposing when sewing rows together. Add inside border. Check to ensure the quilt center measures exactly 48½".

Sew Swag Border rectangles together into four groups of four blocks. Press seams open. The border should measure exactly 48½". If it does not, adjust seams between border blocks. Add 6½" background cornerstones to the ends of two groups of four making two 60½" borders.

Stitch the two 48½" Swag Borders to the sides of the quilt center. Press to the small inner border.

Stitch the two 60½" Swag Borders to the top and bottom of the quilt center. Press to the small inner border.

Step I - Quilt Finishing

Make a backing. Layer quilt top, batting, and backing. Baste and quilt as desired. Square up your quilt, bind, label, and enjoy!

DIAGRAM 1 HEART WREATH

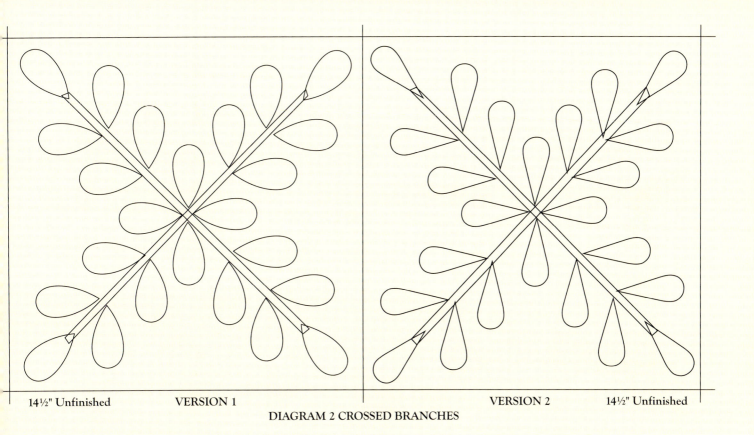

14½" Unfinished VERSION 1 VERSION 2 14½" Unfinished

DIAGRAM 2 CROSSED BRANCHES

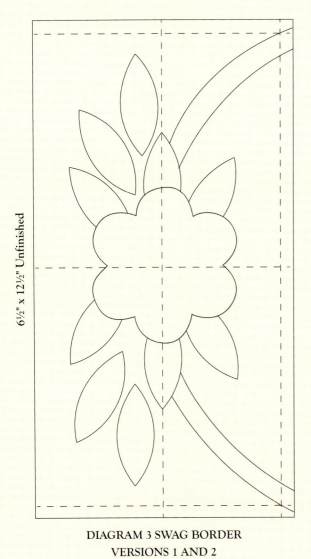

6½" x 12½" Unfinished

DIAGRAM 3 SWAG BORDER
VERSIONS 1 AND 2

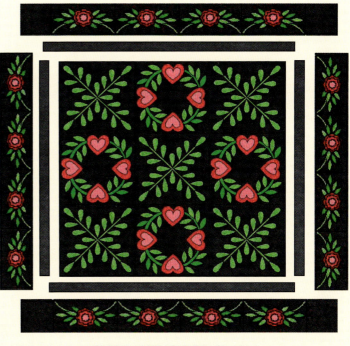

QUILT ASSEMBLY DIAGRAM 4
VERSIONS 1 AND 2

Row Quilt
40" x 54" | Quilt made by Sue Pelland and Joanne Bertrand | Quilted by Linda Gosselin

PROJECT 9: Row Quilt

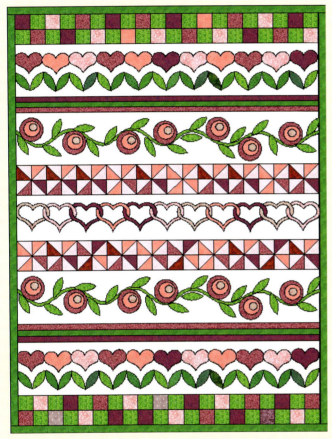

Row 1: Checkerboard

Row 2: Heart Flowers

Row 3: Strips

Row 4: Lollipop Flowers

Row 5: Pinwheels

Row 6: Interlocking Hearts

Row 7: Pinwheels

Row 8: Lollipop Flowers

Row 9: Strips

Row 10: Heart Flowers

Row 11: Checkerboard

DIAGRAM 1

MATERIALS LIST

Fabric 1: 1¼ yards background (white)

Fabric 2: 1 yard for pieced blocks, appliqué leaves and vines (green)

Fabric 3: ¾ yard light fabric (light pink)

Fabric 4: ¾ yard medium fabric (medium pink)

Fabric 5: ¾ yard dark fabric (dark pink)

Fusible web: 4 yards, 20" wide Mistyfuse

Backing: 2½ yards

Binding: ⅓ yard

Batting: 45" x 60"

ASSEMBLY INSTRUCTIONS

Step A: Wash and Press all Fabric

Step B: Precut and Prepare Fabrics

Fabric 1: Background Fabric (white in example)
   Cut four 7½" x WOF strips for
   Rows 2, 4, 8 and 10
   Cut one 6½" x WOF strip for Row 6

Fabric 2: Leaf Fabric
   Cut three 2½" x WOF strips for Step C
   Cut two 1½" x WOF strips for Step E

Fabric 3: Light Flower Fabric (light pink in example)
   Cut one 2½" x WOF strips for Step C
   Cut ten 6" squares for Step D

Fabric 4: Medium Flower Fabric (medium pink in example)
   Cut one 2½" x WOF strips for Step C
   Cut five 6" squares for Step D
   Cut four 1½" x WOF strips for Step E

Fabric 5: Dark Flower Fabric (dark pink in example)
   Cut one 2½" x WOF strips for Step C
   Cut five 6" squares for Step D

From leftover Fabric 2 to 5: Put fusible on the back of fabric after precutting strips and squares.

Step C: Make Two Checkerboard Rows (Rows 1 and 11)

Sew three strips sets, one each of Fabric 2 and 3, 2 and 4, 2 and 5. Press all seams toward Fabric 2. Cross cut strip sets into 2½" strips. Arrange in a checkerboard pattern as shown in the example. Make two checkerboard rows with twenty pairs in each row.

Step D: Make Two Pinwheel Rows (Rows 5 and 7)

Put two 6" fabric squares right sides together using Fabric 3 in each pair. (make ten) Draw a diagonal line from corner to corner in both directions. Sew ¼" on both sides of the diagonal lines. Cut the block into four 3" squares, then cut on the diagonal lines making eight half-square triangles from each pair of 6" squares. (Photo 1)

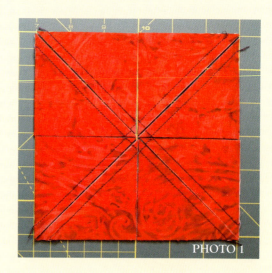
PHOTO 1

Press seams away from the Fabric 3. Square up the half square triangles to measure 2½". Make 80 half square triangles. (Photo 2)

PHOTO 2

Sew four half-square triangles together to make a pinwheel block. Sew ten pinwheel blocks together to make each row. Make two pinwheel rows.

Step E: Make Two Strip Rows (Rows 3 and 9)

Sew the 1½" strips of Fabric 2 and Fabric 4 together with Fabric 2 in the center. Press away from the center strip. Repeat to make two strip sets.

Step F: Make Two Lollipop Flower Rows (Rows 4 and 8)

From Fabric 5 cut fourteen 3" circles.

From Fabric 4 cut fourteen 2" circles.

From Fabric 3 cut fourteen 1" circles.

Note: Mark and cut the 1" circles with scissors.

Keeping each circle off center, press the dark fabric to your appliqué pressing sheet. Press the 2" circle off center on the 3" circle. Press the 1" circle off center again. Remove the three part lollipop flower from the pressing sheet. (Photo 3)

PHOTO 3

Cut 3/8" bias strips from a 14" square of green fused fabric to make the curved vine. You will only need a few strips, so cut them from corner to corner to make them as long as possible. (Photo 4)

PHOTO 4

If using Leaves Galore Norme template, cut vines from fused green strip 41" x 2½". Fold strip in half. Line up the small "a" in the center of the 3" curved edge on the fold. Cut using the 3" curve. Slide template over by 3/8" and cut again keeping the "a" on the fold.

Cut 78 - 3" standard leaves with Hearts and More Template C, large end, 40 to 40 degrees on fold. Use 34 for the lollipop flower row and 44 for the heart flower rows. It is faster to use the Leaves Galore Norme template to make the 3" leaves for both rows if you have this tool.

Assembly of Lollipop Flowers Row: Using a 7½" background strip, mark a chalk line or fold the 7½" strip down the center and finger press. Trace the dashed vine pattern on the background fabric using an iron-erase pen such as the Frixion pen. Center the bias strip or the curve cut with the 3" Leaves Galore template over the dashed line and fuse in place following the curve. Add three piece lollipop flowers along the vine keeping the vine showing either above or below the flower. This will simplify the decorative stitching of the vine. Add leaves along the vine making sure to cover any splices in the vine. (Photo 5)

PHOTO 5

Step G: Make One Linked Hearts Row (Row 6)

Cut three or four hearts from Fabrics 3, 4, and 5 for a total of eleven rings as follows:

Using Hearts and More Template B, large end, place the curved edge of the template on your right and the 90 degree marking and the letter 'm' on the fold. (Photo 6) Once you cut around the template, keep the heart folded.

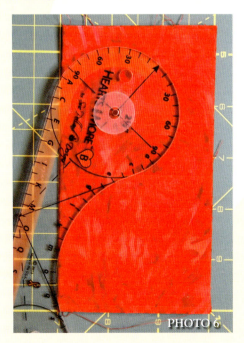
PHOTO 6

Now flip Template B over so that the small end is centered inside the half heart shape. Again, keep the small letter "m" on the fold, but center the smaller circle inside the larger circle that was just cut. Use your eye to keep the space around the small circle even. Cut from the small "m" to the top of the circle. (Photo 7)

The inside heart is a bonus heart that you can use in Rows 1 and 5.

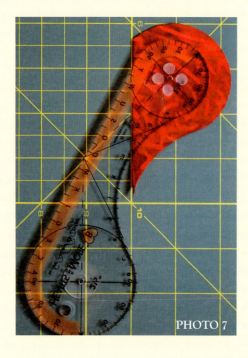

Assembly of Linked Hearts Row: On the 6½" x WOF background strip, measure 1¼" from the top and bottom edge and mark a chalk line or crease using a Hera Marker. Fold the WOF in half to mark the center of the width. Lay out one heart ring directly in the center of the row. Place additional hearts on each side of this center heart overlapping hearts so the inside cuts barely touch. (Photo 8)

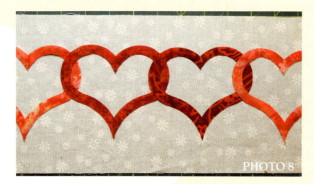

Once all hearts are in place, go back and lift the right edge of each heart and place it over the heart to its right. Starting on the left edge, locate the point where the first two hearts overlap. Cut the top heart (Photo 9) then tuck the cut ends under the heart to the right making them link. Keep the inside cut lines barely touching and make sure the cut ring edges abut one another under the top ring. Fuse each heart in place as you cut and link the hearts together. Only press the left half of the second heart allowing you to link the right side to the next one in line.

Step H: Make Two Heart Flower Rows (Rows 2 and 10)

Use eleven bonus hearts from Row 3, then cut eleven additional hearts using Template B, small end. Use one of the bonus hearts as your guide to keep a consistent size. (Photo 10) Use a total of 22 small hearts for the two rows and 44 leaves cut in Step F.

Assembly of Heart Flower Row: Using the 7½" × WOF strips, measure 1¼" from the top, bottom, and sides of each row. Mark with an iron-erase marker or a Hera Marker. Mark the center of the WOF as well. Starting in the center of the row, place the small hearts so the side edges touch and the top edges fall on the top line 1¼" down from the top of the fabric. Having the edges touch makes stitching around the hearts easier. You can put a bit of space between the hearts if you wish, but you will have to pull your thread ends through to the back on every heart.

Place the 3" leaves in a "V" shape under each heart, keeping the bottom of the "V" on the 1¼" line on the bottom of the row and the top of the "V" on the center line. Try to keep the top points and the bottom points on the leaves touching to make a zigzag. This will also help make stitching easier with no stopping and starting. (Photo 16)

Step I: Stitch Appliqué

Stitch around all green stems and leaves with a matching thread. Stitch around all flower colors in a matching thread. We used 100 weight Invisifil thread from Wonderfil.

We chose a very small zigzag stitch to finish the raw edges. The Invisifil blends right into the appliqué fabrics so the stitching is not very noticeable.

Step J: Assemble the Appliqué Rows Together with Pieced Rows

Arrange strip sets in any order, using the linked hearts in the middle of the quilt. Trim all rows to 40½" length. Sew all rows together using ¼" seams. Press away from the appliqué rows.

Step K: Quilt Finishing

Make a backing. Layer quilt top, batting, and backing. Baste and quilt as desired. Square up your quilt, bind, label, and enjoy!

Variations: You can follow my example exactly or you can use any combination of rows to make your quilt unique. See the examples below.

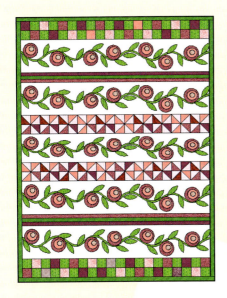
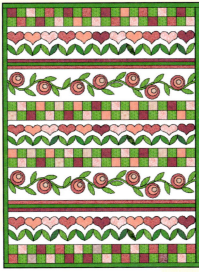

Appendix

STRAIGHT-EDGE HEART

Template	End(in)	Smallest Straight-Edge Heart Cutting Instructions	Smallest Straight-Edge Heart W x H(in)	Largest Straight-Edge Heart Cutting Instructions	Largest Straight-Edge Heart W x H(in)
A	1	90° to T	$1^7/_8 \times 1^1/_4$	70° to E	3×2
A	$1^5/_8$	90° to M	3×2	70° to Y	$3^1/_2 \times 3^1/_8$
B	$1^3/_4$	90° to T	$3^1/_8 \times 2^1/_4$	70° to C	$5^5/_8 \times 3^1/_2$
B	$2^1/_2$	90° to K	$4^1/_2 \times 3^1/_8$	70° to Y	$6 \times 4^3/_4$
C	2	90° to T	$3^1/_2 \times 2^3/_4$	70° to C	$7^3/_8 \times 3^7/_8$
C	4	90° to N	$7^1/_4 \times 4^7/_8$	80° to Y	$7^3/_8 \times 7^7/_8$
D	3	90° to S	$5^3/_8 \times 4$	70° to G	$8^1/_4 \times 5^3/_8$
D	5	90° to O	$9^1/_2 \times 6^3/_4$	80° to Y	$10^3/_8 \times 9^3/_4$

CURVED-EDGE HEART

Template	End(in)	Smallest Curved-Edge Heart Cutting Instructions	Smallest Curved-Edge Heart W x H(in)	Largest Curved-Edge Heart Cutting Instructions	Largest Curved-Edge Heart W x H(in)
A	1	Z to l	$1^3/_4 \times 1^1/_2$	Z to j	$1^3/_4 \times 1^3/_4$
A	$1^5/_8$	A to m	$2^7/_8 \times 2^1/_2$	90° to m	$2^3/_4 \times 2^1/_2$
B	$1^3/_4$	Z to n	$3^1/_4 \times 2^1/_2$	Z to l	$3^1/_4 \times 3$
B	$2^1/_2$	90° to i	$4^1/_8 \times 3$	90° to m	$4^3/_8 \times 3^7/_8$
C	2	Z to p	$3^1/_2 \times 2^1/_2$	90° to m	$3^3/_8 \times 3^1/_4$
C	4	A to k	$6^7/_8 \times 4^3/_4$	A to n	$7 \times 5^5/_8$
D	3	Z to n	$5^1/_4 \times 4$	Z to l	$5^1/_2 \times 4^7/_8$
D	5	A to l	$8^3/_4 \times 6^1/_2$	A to m	$8^3/_4 \times 7$

FLOWER PETAL (STRAIGHT-EDGE TEARDROP)

Template	End(in)	Smallest Flower Petal Cutting Instructions	Smallest Flower Petal W x H(in)	Largest Flower Petal Cutting Instructions	Largest Flower Petal W x H(in)
A	1	0° to U	$1\frac{1}{4} \times \frac{3}{4}$	0° to E	$3\frac{1}{8} \times 1\frac{3}{8}$
A	$1\frac{5}{8}$	10° orange to K	$2\frac{1}{8} \times 1\frac{1}{4}$	10° orange to Z	$3\frac{5}{8} \times 2$
B	$1\frac{3}{4}$	0° to U	$2 \times 1\frac{1}{4}$	0° to E	$5\frac{3}{8} \times 2$
B	$2\frac{1}{2}$	0° to G	$2\frac{3}{4} \times 1\frac{7}{8}$	0° to Y	$6\frac{1}{4} \times 3$
C	2	0° to U	$2\frac{3}{4} \times 1\frac{5}{8}$	0° o H	$6\frac{1}{4} \times 2\frac{1}{4}$
C	4	0° to K	$4\frac{3}{4} \times 3\frac{1}{2}$	10° orange to Y	$8\frac{1}{4} \times 4\frac{1}{4}$
D	3	0° to U	$3\frac{3}{4} \times 2\frac{3}{8}$	10° orange to H	$8 \times 3\frac{1}{4}$
D	5	0° orange to I	$5\frac{1}{2} \times 3\frac{5}{8}$	10° orange to Y	$10\frac{7}{8} \times 5\frac{1}{8}$

LEAF

Template	End(in)	Smallest Leaf Cutting Instructions	Smallest Leaf W x H(in)	Largest Leaf Cutting Instructions	Largest Leaf W x H(in)
A	1	50° to 50°	$\frac{7}{8} \times \frac{3}{8}$	70° to 70°	$1 \times \frac{5}{8}$
A	$1\frac{5}{8}$	40° to 40°	$1\frac{1}{8} \times \frac{3}{8}$	70° to 70°	$1\frac{5}{8} \times 1$
B	$1\frac{3}{4}$	40° to 40°	$1\frac{1}{8} \times \frac{3}{8}$	60° to 60°	$1\frac{1}{2} \times \frac{7}{8}$
B	$2\frac{1}{2}$	30° to 30°	$1\frac{3}{8} \times \frac{3}{8}$	60° to 60°	$2\frac{1}{4} \times 1\frac{1}{4}$
C	2	40° to 40°	$1\frac{3}{8} \times \frac{1}{2}$	60° to 60°	$1\frac{3}{4} \times 1$
C	4	30° to 30°	$2 \times \frac{1}{2}$	60° to 60°	$3\frac{1}{2} \times 2$
D	3	30° to 30°	$1\frac{1}{2} \times \frac{3}{8}$	60° to 60°	$2\frac{5}{8} \times 1\frac{1}{2}$
D	5	30° to 30°	$2\frac{5}{8} \times \frac{5}{8}$	60° to 60°	$4\frac{3}{8} \times 2\frac{1}{2}$

OVAL

Template	End(in)	Size of rectangle W x H(in)	Smallest Oval Cutting Instructions	Smallest Oval W x H(in)	Size of rectangle W x H(in)	Largest Oval Cutting Instructions	Largest Oval W x H(in)
A	1	2¼ x 1½	20° to W	1⅝ x 1	6½ x 1½	20° to E	6 x 1
A	1⅝	2¼ x 1¾	40° to E	1⅞ x 1¼	7¼ x 2¼	30° to X	6¾ x 1½
B	1¾	2½ x 2	30° to Y	2 x 1½	11¾ x 2	30° to C	11¼ x 1½
B	2½	4 x 3	30° to E	3½ x 2½	12½ x 3¼	20° to Y	11⅞ x 2⅞
C	2	3¼ x 3	30° to X	2⅞ x 1½	14½ x 3	10° to D	14 x 2½
C	4	6 x 4	40° to G	5⅝ x 3⅝	16 x 4¾	30° to Y	15½ x 4¼
D	3	5¼ x 3	30° to W	4¾ x 2½	19¼ x 3¾	20° to D	18¾ x 3⅜
D	5	6½ x 4¾	40° to E	5⅞ x 4¼	21¼ x 5¾	30° to Y	20¾ x 5¼

FLOWER

Template	End(in)	Size of square W x H(in)	Smallest Flower Cutting Instructions	Smallest Flower W x H(in)	Size of square W x H(in)	Largest Flower Cutting Instructions	Largest Flower W x H(in)
A	1	2½ x 2½	60° to 60°	1⅞ x 1⅞	3 x 3	90° to 90°	2¾ x 2¾
A	1⅝	4 x 4	70° to 70°	3¾ x 3¾	5 x 5	90° to 90°	4½ x 4½
B	1¾	5 x 5	70° to 70°	4⅛ x 4⅛	5½ x 5½	90° to 90°	4⅞ x 4⅞
B	2½	6 x 6	60° to 60°	5 x 5	7½ x 7½	90° to 90°	6¾ x 6¾
C	2	5½ x 5½	70° to 70°	4⅝ x 4⅝	6 x 6	90° to 90°	5½ x 5½
C	4	8½ x 8½	60° to 60°	8 x 8	11½ x 11½	90° to 90°	10⅞ x 10⅞
D	3	6 x 6	50° to 50°	5⅛ x 5⅛	9½ x 9½	90° to 90°	7⅜ x 7⅜
D	5	12 x 12	70° to 70°	11⅜ x 11⅜	15 x 15	90° to 90°	13½ x 13½

WATER DROPLET (CURVED-EDGE TEARDROP)

Template	End(in)	Smallest Water Droplet Cutting Instructions	Smallest Water Droplet W x H(in)	Largest Water Droplet Cutting Instructions	Largest Water Droplet W x H(in)
A	1	30° orange to o	1¼ × ⅞	30° orange to l	1⅝ × ⅞
A	1⅝	10° orange to h	1⅞ × 1¼	30° to j	2¼ × 1⅝
B	1¾	10° clear to o	2¼ × 1⅛	30° to n	2⅝ × 1⅞
B	2½	0° to g	2¾ × 1¾	30° to k	3¾ × 2¾
C	2	10° clear to q	2¼ × 1⅛	30° to n	3 × 2
C	4	0° to i	4½ × 2⅞	30° to k	5¼ × 4¼
D	3	0° to o	3¾ × 2	30° to n	4½ × 3
D	5	0° to j	6 × 3⅝	30° to k	6¾ × 5¼

DRUNKARD'S PATH

Drunkard's Path Template size	Cut size of dark square(in)	For every dark square cut two light squares(in)	Cut size of second light square and Mistyfuse(in)	Makes unfinished block size(in)	How many blocks does it make?
Template D: 5"	8¼	8¼	6	4	4 light 4 dark
Template C: 4"	6¾	6¾	5	3¼	4 light 4 dark
Template D: 3"	5¼	5¼	4	2½	4 light 4 dark
Template C: 2"	3¾	3¾	2¾	1¾	4 light 4 dark

Note: When trimming squares to the final unfinished block size, trim only the background fabric, not the quarter circle.

TILE QUILTS

Tile Block finished size(in)	Cut size of dark square with Mistyfuse on the back(in)	For every dark square cut two light squares(in)	Cut two corners of dark square with this template from zero to 90°	How many blocks does it make?
8	8½	8½	D, 5"	1 light center 1 dark center
7	7½	7½	D, 5"	1 light center 1 dark center
6	6½	6½	C, 4"	1 light center 1 dark center
5	5½	5½	C, 4"	1 light center 1 dark center
4	4½	4½	D, 3"	1 light center 1 dark center
3	2½	2½	B, 2½"	1 light center 1 dark center

LEAVES GALORE LEAVES TRIMMED WITH HEARTS AND MORE TEMPLATES

Size of Leaves Galore Leaf	Trim with Hearts and More Template
2½" Petite	A Small 60° to 60° *
3" Norme	A Small 60° to 60° *
4" Grande	B Small 70° to 70° C Small 70° to 70°
5" Petite	A Large 60° to 60° B Small 70° to 70°
6" Norme	B Small 70° to 70° C Small 90° to 90°
8" Grande	B large 70° to 70° D small 60° to 60°

- These leaves are small, so there is only one good way to trim them. Larger leaves have more options for trimming. Two options are shown for each leaf size starting at the 4" Leaves Galore leaf. Examples are shown on page 35. (Photo 23 and 24)

Patterns

Enlarge 125% on copier. Line up red lines on pages 97 and 98.

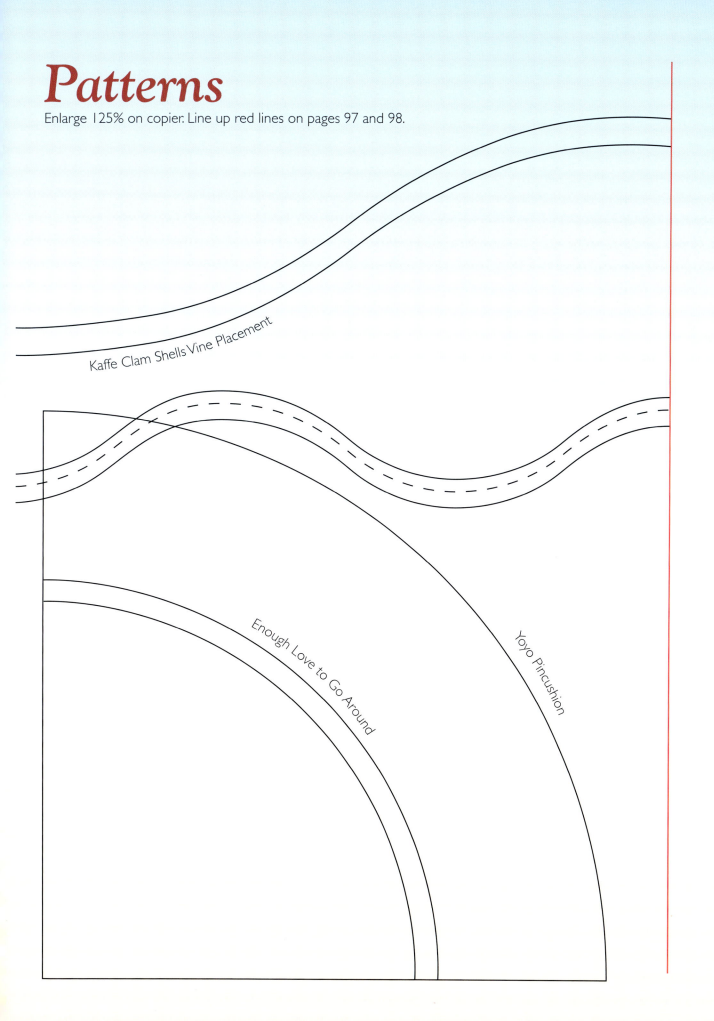

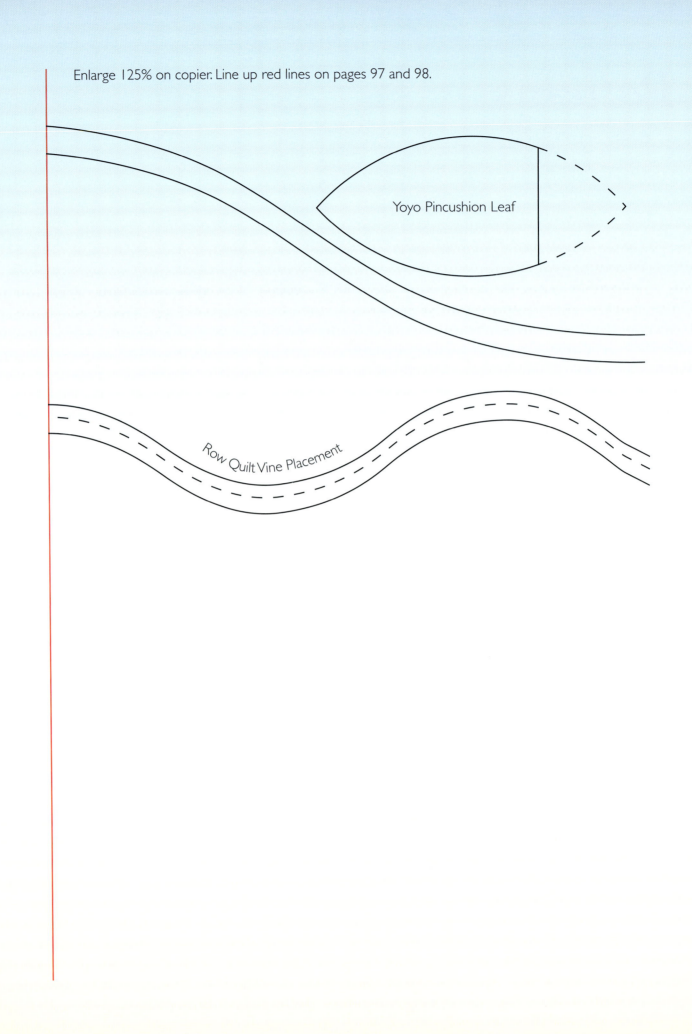

Resources

A free video demonstration of the Hearts and More templates, Leaves Galore templates, and the Quilter's Chalk Line are available at suepellanddesigns.com. These demonstrations are intended to help you learn how to use the templates. New video demonstrations will be added periodically. Like us on Facebook, and sign up for our newsletter to be kept informed of new patterns, books, videos, tools and techniques.

The shop at suepellanddesigns.com offers patterns, templates, and my favorite tools used in this book. Hearts and More patterns pictured in this book, Mistyfuse, and all recommended tools are available from suepellanddesigns.com including:

HM1SM	Hearts and More™ Small Set
HM2LG	Hearts and More™ Large Set
HM3ST	Hearts and More™ Set of four
SPD301	Unchain My Heart, a Hearts and More pattern
SPD302	Jasmine, a Hearts and More pattern
SPD303	He Loves Me! a Hearts and More pattern
SPD304	Bouquet, a Hearts and More pattern
SPD305	Conversation Hearts, a Hearts and More pattern
SPD306	Spin Me Round, a Hearts and More pattern
MAT001	Matilda Rotating Cutting Mat

If you are a quilt designer and would like to use my templates in your patterns, please refer to "Hearts and More Templates" by name and put a link to my website in your pattern.

Professional Machine Quilters who added their artistry to quilts in this book include:

Katherine Amadon

Diana Reinhardt Annis
Norton, MA

Kathy Sperino
Finishing Lines
Mendon, MA
finishinglinesbyksperino.blogspot.com

Debbie Wendt
Wendt Quilting
Uxbridge, MA
wendtquilting.com

Linda Gosselin
Quilters Help Desk
Northbridge, MA

Thank you to our quilt makers:

Susan Arena
Joanne Bertrand
Donna Bozeman

Beth Helfter
Donna Hopkins
Akiko Kunst

Elaine Nadeau
Antoinette Riskalla
Nancy Sullivan

Additional resources and products used in this book:

Susan Cleveland
Pieces Be With You
Piping Hot Binding tool and other wonderful tools and instructions
www.piecesbewithyou.com

Deb Wendt
Wendt Quilting
Brilliant Bindings tool and excellent patterns
Wendtquiting.com

About the Author

In the 1980s, when I was in high school, my Mom and I decided to open a quilt shop. Back then we did every inch of our cutting, piecing, appliqué and quilting by hand. Yet we were on the cusp of a new era in quilting. Being young and wanting instant gratification, I learned everything I could about newly invented strip piecing methods, rotary cutting, and fusibles from innovators in the field. I took every class I could on my quest to find better, faster, and more accurate ways to make quilts.

Soon I developed a love of appliqué. Instead of persnickety perfectly pieced blocks, I could create a garden full of flowers in the midst of our long New England winters. Appliqué wasn't all about accuracy, it was about beauty. That was where I wanted to put my creative energies rather than striving for perfect points.

For four years after high school, I worked in our shop while I studied Textile Chemistry in college. As soon as I graduated, I landed my dream job working as a chemist for Cranston Print Works Company. It was a pleasure being surrounded by millions of yards of fabric at work and I never got tired of the sight, smell, and sounds of the mill. Cranston never realized the extent of my addiction and for five glorious years they enabled this fabriholic to collect as much fabric as I pleased.

Soon I was married with three kids and anxious to get out of the house now and then. I turned to quilting as my favorite form of "Mommy time". My local guild whittled, carved, and polished my skills as a quilter and for that I am eternally grateful.

Leaves Galore took me by surprise. One day when designing a quilt for a guild challenge, I realized I had to cut hundreds of small leaves. I knew there wasn't enough time to appliqué all those leaves before the challenge quilts were revealed so I turned to fusible appliqué: fusing, tracing, and cutting hundreds of fusible leaves. There had to be a better way. Then one night the light bulb in my head went on....Leaves Galore was born.

Five years later, I wanted more appliqué shapes to play with. I developed Hearts and More to complement the shapes that Leaves Galore could cut. Using both templates together expanded my appliqué abilities.

Since developing Leaves Galore over eight years ago, I have found teaching to be the most rewarding part of my job. I love showing others how simple and effective my methods are. Through my two books, YouTube, and my website I am able to teach quilters all over the globe. Even if we never get to meet in person, I hope my passion for my tools and methods comes through these pages and encourages you to try, succeed, and fall in love with Rotary Cut Appliqué.